WITHDRAWN

HARVARD LIBRARY

WITHDRAWN

REINCARNATION
AND JUDAISM

REINCARNATION AND JUDAISM

THE JOURNEY OF THE SOUL

DovBer Pinson

A Jason Aronson Book

ROWMAN & LITTLEFIELD PUBLISHERS, INC.
Lanham • Boulder • New York • Toronto • Oxford

A JASON ARONSON BOOK

ROWMAN & LITTLEFIELD PUBLISHERS, INC.

Published in the United States of America
by Rowman & Littlefield Publishers, Inc.
A wholly owned subsidiary of The Rowman & Littlefield Publishing Group, Inc.
4501 Forbes Boulevard, Suite 200, Lanham, Maryland 20706
www.rowmanlittlefield.com

PO Box 317
Oxford
OX2 9RU, UK

Copyright © 1999 by DovBer Pinson
First Rowman & Littlefield edition 2004

All rights reserved. No part of this publication may be reproduced, stored in a retrieval system, or transmitted in any form or by any means, electronic, mechanical, photocopying, recording, or otherwise, without the prior permission of the publisher.

British Library Cataloguing in Publication Information Available

Library of Congress Cataloging-in-Publication Data

Pinson, DovBer, 1971–
    Reincarnation & Judaism—the journey of the soul. By DovBer Pinson.
        p. cm.
    Includes bibliographical references and index.
    ISBN 0-7657-6064-9
    1. Transmigration—Judaism. 2. Soul (Judaism) 3. Cabala. I. Title.
BM635.7.P56 1999
296.3'3—dc21   98-42260
                                                            CIP

Printed in the United States of America

♾™ The paper used in this publication meets the minimum requirements of American National Standard for Information Sciences—Permanence of Paper for Printed Library Materials, ANSI/NISO Z39.48-1992.

Contents

Introduction	1
The Soul and Its Eternity	25
The Purpose of the Soul's Descent	49
The Afterlife of the Soul	63
Reincarnation as Punishment or *Tikkun*	79
Different Forms of Reincarnation: *Ibbur* and Dybbuk	107
Can We Remember Our Previous Incarnations?	125
Can Reincarnation Be Proven?	137
Kabbalah and Philosophy: Parallels and Distinctions	157
Debating Reincarnation: Common Arguments Against Reincarnation and the Response	183
Appendix	187

Preface

There was once a poor simple man eking out a meager existence in his hometown, the small village of Lodz. Zalman led a very ordinary life, much like the other villagers, save for one thing. For months now, Zalman had been having a recurring dream in which he was told that in the distant city of Prague, under the Charles Bridge leading to the castle, lay great treasure, unlike anything he had ever seen or imagined. Zalman brushed the dream off at first, only to become more and more convinced as the vision appeared to him night after night. Finally, he decided to brave the journey to the distant land of Prague. Upon his arrival, he immediately inquired as to the location of the Charles Bridge. He hurried with great eagerness and excitement, and finally stood before the great bridge. Under the bridge, Zalman could see an old, bedraggled man, sitting directly on the spot he had seen so vividly in his dreams. Zalman spoke to the man, and requested that the man move. The man refused and Zalman, at a loss, offered the man a portion of the treasure he would discover. Upon hearing this the man began to laugh. "I too know of a treasure from my dreams," he said. "I have a recurring dream for years now, that in a small town called Lodz, directly beneath the home of a man called Zalman, lies great buried treasure!" And it all became clear to Zalman. He realized that he had traveled so far only to find that the treasure had always been within his reach, only awaiting his retrieval.

When we hear of mysticism and ethereal notions, we imagine distant lands, foreign cultures, and exotic locations. We don't think to seek it in our own home. We wander and search for those distant treasures, not realizing that they were in our reach all along.

In this book, we will uncover some of the most beautiful treasures of mysticism—Jewish mysticism. The idea of reincarnation is replete with misconceptions, beginning with the very source of the notion which so many mistakenly believe to be a foreign, unJewish idea. Reincarnation, in fact, is deeply rooted in Jewish thought, from the ancient Kabbalists to modern Chasidic philosophy. Reincarnation was, and continues to be, a fundamental tenet in Jewish belief.

My rebbe, the Lubavitcher Rebbe of blessed memory, may his merits serve to protect us, once related a story:

> A great Rabbi who possessed scores of devoted and learned *chasidim*, many of them great in their own right, once befriended a simple man, unlearned and unremarkable in any way, and accorded him much honor and affection. This puzzled many of the *chasidim*, and finally, one chasid, a righteous and learned man, dared approach the Rebbe with this concern. The Rebbe did not reply. A few days later, he requested that this chasid, who was a diamond merchant of great expertise, bring him some samples of diamonds to view. The diamond merchant-

chasid came as requested, bringing with him a collection of the most exquisite stones. The Rebbe asked him about each stone. The man proceeded to display the diamonds and name the prices for each one. "This one is worth 100 rubles, this one is worth 500 rubles," and withdrawing a diamond from the bottom of his display he proclaimed, "This one is worth 2000 rubles!" The Rebbe shrugged and said, "With all due respect, Yankel, the 500 ruble diamond looks exactly like the 2000 ruble diamond, if not more glittering and beautiful." The merchant said, "In all modesty, Rebbe, to truly appreciate the value of a diamond one must be an expert." The Rebbe gave him a broad smile in return. "Yes, Yankele, that is so. And to truly appreciate the quality of a *neshoma*, a soul, one must also be an expert!"

We look at another person and we see the superficial, the external. Yet hidden beneath the physicality exist layers of spirituality. The soul is more multifaceted than the most precious of diamonds, containing within it centuries of incarnations, layers of accomplishments, good deeds, and inspirations. Each incarnation has contributed to the soul, leaving it each time more elevated, more complete than it was before. Within each of us lies a soul more complex and holy than we can imagine.

The issues dealt with in this book are deep and intricate, yet my desire is to speak to every mind piqued by this fascinating yet mystifying concept. Towards this end, I have attempted to explain these complex issues in basic terms. It is my hope that you will find enrichment and inspiration within the treasures beneath you, the mystical jewels which are our inheritance and our privilege.

—DovBer Pinson

Introduction

The Torah states, "These are the laws of the Torah, *a man*. . . ."[1] Man and the Torah are analogous, for man is likened to the Torah, and the Torah to man. Man is a combination of body and soul, a fusion of matter and spirit. Man has external characteristics, physical features, in addition to his internal quintessence, soul and spirit, which together form this single organism called 'man.' The same is true with the Torah. The Torah contains within it two aspects: the revealed components, the *Niglah*, those parts of the Torah that concern the deeds of man, the laws of the Torah and the manner in which one should conduct himself in this physical world; and as part of the same 'body,' there is the Soul of the Torah, the *Nistar*, the inner components of the Torah, the mystical insights of the law, and the deeper insights into creation.[2]

---

1. *Numbers*, chapter 19, verse 12.
2. *Zohar* part 3, p. 152A.

Through contemplating on these parts of the Torah, one comes to know and understand the greatness of his Creator (as much as humans are capable of comprehending). In addition, through studying about God's greatness and comprehending the vastness of His Being, we will *automatically* experience an appropriate fear of God and sense of awe. Furthermore, we can understand, following our contemplation, Who it is that we fear and for what reason we fear Him.[3]

Once we achieve the proper reverence and awe of God, we can then truly do what God wants. As the Mishnah says, "Affirm My kingdom, and then I will command you on what to do."[4]

As a result, these two components of the holy Torah form *one* unified Torah, as *one body*. Moreover, both were given to man at the same time and place, on Mount Sinai. At Sinai there was a revelation of Torah, with both its characteristics. On one hand, God gave the literal Torah (the Ten commandments, which encompasses within it the entire Torah), which tells us, "Man shall not kill, Man shall not steal," the simple moral and mundane law; and yet, at that very same moment, there was the highest revelation of Godliness that mankind has ever experienced.

---

3. See Rabbi Shalom Dovber (the fifth Chabad Rebbe), *Kuntres Eitz Hayim* (New York: Kehot Publication Society, 1976); Rudolf Otto, in *The Idea Of The Holy* (London: Oxford University Press, 1958), argues that the first step in a religious experience is a sense of awe and marvel of God; also see *Zahot* part 1. p. 7b. Talmud Shabbat 311. Rabbi Schneur Zalman of Liadi, *Tanya* (New York: Kehot Publication Society, 1965) chapter 41.

4. See, *Berachot*, chapter 2, Mishnah, 1.

As it is stated in the Bible, "the notion of Israel . . . saw the sounds."[5] Kabbalah[6] explains that the difference between saying we saw something, or saying we heard about it, is if the object we are speaking of is either close, or far from us. When we say we saw a beautiful painting, this means to say that we were close enough to actually see it; however, when we say we heard of a beautiful painting, it means we were never close enough to actually see it, we only heard of it.

When we speak of physical objects, we can state that we saw the object; however, when speaking of spirituality, we speak of it as if from a distance. We can only say we heard of it. We cannot see spirituality, we can only speak of it. Nevertheless, at Mount Sinai, man experienced spirituality with such proximity, it was as if he *saw it*, for Sinai was the ultimate and preeminent revelation of Godliness to man. It was at that moment, when we received the mystical insights of the revealed parts of the Torah, that we *saw* mysticism.

Both these components, the law and the spirit behind the law are extremely important, for if we only have the law—

---

5. *Exodus*, chapter 20, verse 15. See *Rashi* [abbrev. Rabbi Shlomo Yitzhaki], pp. 1040–1105), *Mechilta* on this verse. See also *Targum Yonathan Ben Uziel*. Ad loc.

6. The Lubavitcher Rebbe, Rabbi M. M. Schneerson, *Likutei Sichot* (New York: Kehot Publication Society, 1972) Vol. 6, Parshat Yitro (2) p. 121; Rabbi Schneur Zalman of Liadi, *Torah Or* (New York: Kehot Publication Society, 1996), p. 63. Rabbi Chayim of Volozhin (1749–1821) *Nefesh HaChayim* (Bnei Brak: 1989) Shar 3, chapter 11. The simple, rational explanation for the phenomenon—of viewing sounds—is explained as follows. Just like when it is cold, the words you utter create a visible effect, at the giving of the Torah, a thick dark cloud descended upon Mount Sinai, causing the words of God to be seen. See Rabbi Bachya Ibn Pakudah (1050–1120), *Torat HaNefesh* (Paris: 1896), chapter 3. See also: Rabbi Meir Ben Gabbai (1480–1547) *Tola'at Ya'akov* (Jerusalem: Makot Chayim, 1967) p. 33.

the external, the body—without the soul (although then we can know exactly what God want us to do), we would then be connected and permeated with Godliness only on the level of functional consciousness, meaning that although our actions would be devoted to God, Godliness would not permeate *our entire existence*. Our minds and hearts would still be devoid of Godliness. Even though God desires man to connect himself with Godliness in his actions, the ultimate purpose of man's creation is (as will be further explained) that he should draw Godliness down into the most physical of things, and, even more, he should transform the entire physical reality into the spiritual. Not only in the world at large should Godliness be revealed, but also in his personal world—his body. His entire physical existence shall metamorphose into a Godly being, not only his actions and intellect, rather, his entire being shall become actively, intellectually, and emotionally connected with Godliness.[7] Thus, it is essential that there is the inner dimensions of the Torah, the parts of the Torah that speak overtly of God, to arouse and inspire one's intellect and emotions to God.

The great Jewish philosopher and codifier Maimonides (Rambam, 1135–1204), writes, "When man will study these aspects of the Torah correctly, he will automatically feel more intimate and close with God, and that will lead him to *love God*."[8] Hence, it is very important to study the spirit behind the law, its inner and mystical dimensions to arouse one's love towards his Creator.

Yet, conversely, only having the spirit of the law, *the intentions behind the law*, without the actual mundane and

---

7. Rabbi M. M. Schneerson, *Likutei Sichot* (New York: Kehot Publication Society, 1980), Vol. 16, p. 477.
8. See *Rambam*. Hilchot Yesodei Hatorah, chapter 4, Halacha 12.

physical law, is also spiritually unhealthy. If there is no actual law that tells man that he should not steal or kill, then eventually there is room for complete chaos. If one's personal intentions are what decide right and wrong, then the line between good and evil begins to blur. Many a person would have Godly intentions for wrongdoings (even the most hideous of deeds), and many would do right without Godly intentions. There would be no absolute definition of good and evil. It is interesting to note that this notion (of only having the spirit behind the law, without the actual law) was actually the first quarrel the Jews were involved in, following the giving of the Torah.

The Torah tells of a disagreement between the Israelites and Moses. The dispute was instigated and led by a man named Korach, well known to be a man of great knowledge[9] and wealth.[10]

For us to fully understand the disagreement, we must preface it with a statement from the Talmud: "The world was created with the letter Hei."[11] Kabbalah[12] explains that, in the letter *Hei*, there are three lines (ה): two connecting lines (the line on the right and the line overhead) and a third line that is not connected. The right and left lines run parallel to each other and end on the same plane. The two attached lines—the right line and the one overhead—represent in man the two closely associated capacities: the intellect of man, which thinks (the line overhead), and his power

---

9. *Midrash Tanchuma* Korach, chapter 2.
10. *Midrash Rabba Exodus* Parsha 31, chapter 3.
11. Talmud, *Menachot* 29b.
12. Rabbi M. M. Schneerson. *Likutei Sichot* (New York: Kehot Publication Society, 1974), Vol. 8, p. 108. See also: Rabbi Schneur Zalman of Liadi "Torah Or," p. 956. "Likkutei Torah" p. 3:67A.

of speech, which actualizes his thoughts (the line to the right). These traits are closely connected to each other, because it is with one's intellect that one thinks the thoughts, and it is with one's speech that one's thoughts are conveyed. Thus, both are used for intellectual purposes. The left line (the disconnected line) is the capacity of action. Just as in the *Hei*, both these lines end on the same plane. This means to say that all one's actions (the left line) are guided by the intellect (the right line), i.e., they can go no further than the intellect will take them.

True intellect is that of the Torah, which is a divine wisdom. Therefore, although a person can, and must, elevate as much of this physical world to holiness as is possible, nevertheless, all his actions must be guided by the law of the Torah, the line to the right.

The first letter in Korach's name is a *Kuf* (ק), which is very similar to the letter *Hei*. The only difference is that, in the Kuf, the line representing the power of action (the left line) ends on a lower plane than that of the line representing the intellect, the law of the Torah (the right line).

We can now understand Korach's disagreement with Moses. Korach came to Moses and said, "If the whole purpose of the law is actually the spirit behind it, and in every commandment there is a deeper purpose which serves to elevate the physical, then why do we need the law? Why have the law with all its limitations and restrictions? Let there be no law that obligates man to do certain actions and forbids other actions. Let us have only the Spirit, the inner dimensions of the law, the intention of the law." In other words, allow the line of action to surpass the line of law, as long as the actions are executed with 'Godly intentions'." Let the individual write his own set of laws decided by his intentions. Why does man need to be dictated by a Divine law?

Moses answered this claim by saying, As humans we must remember that we are but *creations*, and not creators. We are constantly receiving, gathering, and being impressed by external stimuli; and, therefore, are inevitably biased in our decisions. There is no such thing as being a truly objective observer of reality, as seeing things as they really exist; therefore, whatever we, as humans, do, it will always be justified in our own eyes. (The worst murderers in history have had some sort of self-justification for their misdeeds; for example, they felt they were doing something essentially good, for the greater good of society, for religious purposes, and the like.)

For this reason, we must have a Divine law—the revealed parts of the Torah, the parts of the Torah that instruct man as to what he can and cannot do. Without it, there is chaos. "The road to hell is paved with good intentions."[13] Good intention without law leads to anarchy.

From this, we understand the dangers of learning mysticism without being grounded in the actual law. We can observe examples of this in the history of the Jewish people. There were, at various points in history, men who convinced themselves and those around them that they were above good and evil. They claimed that, while the majority of the people are only capable of elevating the physical from within the confines of Jewish Law, they had the unique ability to elevate even the lowliest and most evil of deeds. They believed themselves not only to be capable of this rather, also as responsible for the elevation of evil and impurity for the rest of the people. They proclaimed them-

---

13. See Professor Abraham Joshua Heschel, *God in Search of Man* (New York: The Noonday Press, 1955), p. 293; Aldous Huxley, *The Perennial Philosophy* (Harper Collins, 1990), chapter 18.

selves the Messiah and said that they would bring the redemption through the elevation of impurity, through transgressing the law with Godly intentions. These people caused great misfortune to individuals around them and to the Jewish nation at large, resulting in spiritual confusion and darkness.[14]

How does one do a mitzvah using only the mystical and disregarding the law itself? To understand this, I offer an example: There is a mitzvah to "love your fellow man as yourself."[15] A person studying the inner dimensions of the mitzvah learns that it means, that unification with our fellow man on this earth, causes reactions above and has direct influence on the spiritual worlds.[16] This translates to mean that in the level of Shekinah from which all souls are derived, there is a unificiation caused by one's love for a fellowman. (The unifications above are much needed, for the Shekinah is an intermediary between the upper and the lower worlds. It receives its holines from God and transmits it below. Godliness will only dwell on that which is unified and therefore it is essential that the Shekinah be whole.)

We can take the deeper interpretation of this mitzvah, namely that of loving your fellow man, and translate it into two different reactions. One is the correct way, and that is to react by realizing that because the mitzvah has not only

---

14. See Gershom G. Scholem, *Major Trends in Jewish Mysticism* (New York: Schocken Books, 1961), lecture 8.

15. *Exodus*, chapter 19, verse 18.

16. See Rabbi Menachem Mendel (the Third Chabad Rebbe), *Derech Mitzvotecha* (New York: Kehot Publication Society, 1953), *Mitzvas Ahavas Yisreal*; see also Rabbi Schneur Zalman of Liadi, *Tanya* (New York: Kehot Publication Society, 1965), chapter 32; Rabbi Eliyohu Ben Moshe, Vidas, *Reshit Chochmah* (Brooklyn: 1984), *Shaar Ha'Anavah*, chapter 4.

an effect in this physical world below, rather, it is such a supreme mitzvah that it also affects the worlds above, then the mitzvah must be done with much more excitement and greater enthusiasm. For, when one understands the inner meaning of the mitzvah, it glorifies the actual physical act. The simple act of kindness becomes a lofty and spiritual deed. However, the other reaction one may have, the wrong reaction, will lead one to say, "Since the inner dimension of the mitzvah is the unification of the spiritual in the worlds above, why should I do the physical commandment, and through that affect the spiritual? I will go directly to the spiritual; and attempt to unify the level of Shekinah with all sorts of intentions and meditations and do away with the physical and mundane action of helping and loving someone else." When one learns mysticism and reacts in this way, it is self-destructive and the beginning of one's spiritual downfall.

For this reason, the sages of the Talmud declare that, "A teacher may show a student the insights of the Torah, only if that student is a true God-fearing human being."[17]

Moreover, as the generations regressed spiritually, the rabbis declared that a person should not study the mystical dimensions of the Torah until he reaches the age of 40.[18] This means that only after having reached the physical maturity of 40 years and the intellectual maturity of 40[19] can a person study the Kabbalah, the mystical insights of the Torah, for only then will the study have the proper effect on the student, and cause an appropriate and positive reaction.

---

17. Talmud. *Chagigah* 13a. See also *Rambam*. Hilchot Yesodei Hatorah, chapter 2, Halacha 12. And chapter 4, Halacha 13.

18. See, *Shulchan Aruch*, Yoreh Deah, chapter 246, in the commentary *Shach*.

19. See, Talmud. *Avodah Zarah* 5b. *Avot* chapter 5. Mishnah 22.

Thus, we find throughout our history, that many of the great mystics were also great Halachic authorities.[20] Rabbi Akiva was the greatest sage of the Talmud. The Talmud states that, wherever there is a disagreement between Rabbi Akiva and his contemporaries, the law is always according to Rabbi Akiva.[21] Therefore, he was able to learn the esoteric parts of the Torah and not be affected in a negative sense.

The Talmud relates a story:[22] There were once four talmudic sages who chose to "Enter the Pardes" (the orchard; namely, the mystical realms) to study the hidden insights of the Torah.[23] Three of the four were not fully prepared for this revelation. One was so overwhelmed with the mystical experience that he was never really able to "descend" back into this physical and mundane world. His mind was "trapped" somewhere above. Another sage was so completely overwhelmed that he actually transcended his physical existence and died in spiritual ecstasy. Yet another one was so utterly mystified by the experience that he became an apostate. Only Rabbi Akiva, who was a true Halachic personality, one who understood the inner purpose of the Torah, was able to "enter and exit in peace." Being that he was well grounded in the physical world, he

---

20. Throughout history the masters of mystical thought were also masters of law—halacha—post talmudic scholars, e.g.: Rabbi Hai Gaon (939–1038), Rabbi Moshe ben Nachman Ramban (1194–1270), Rabbi Yoseph Caro (1488–1575), Rabbi Moshe Isserles, Ramah (1530–1572), Rabbi Eliyahu of Vilna, the Vilna Gaon (1720–1797), Rabbi Schneur Zalman of Liadi, the Rav (1745–1813).

21. The Talmud in numerous places, for instance, Talmud *Sanhedrin* 86a.

22. Talmud *Chagigah* 14b.

23. See Rabbi Nathan Ben Yechiel (1035–1106) *HaAruch* (New York: Kohut, 1963). Even in the name of Rabbi Hai Gaon. See Talmud *Chagigah* 14b. Commentaries by *Rashi* and *Rabbeinu Chananel* (990–1055) ad loc.

was able to study the esoteric, the loftiest concepts of the Torah, and immediately afterward practice the most simple and mundane of laws.[24]

True greatness comes with the descent of inspiration into the everyday minutia of life.[25] One may be an artist of great inspiration and skill, yet without the purchase of the proper brush, canvas, and paint, the talent is but an illusion and will never become greatness. The potential for success must be harnessed in the mundane, in order to be fully realized. The mystical experience is mere potential without the practical application of the halacha to ground it. When the mystical combines with the practical, greatness is achieved.

The preconditions (mentioned before) for learning mysticism were especially necessary in days gone by, when most people were able to receive and find inspiration from studying the actual laws of the holy Torah. They were more spiritually attuned. However, as time went on and the generations became increasingly indifferent to spirituality and detached from holiness, the study of the laws of Torah was not a sufficient source of spiritual inspiration for most. The analogy given is that of a sick child. While the child was healthy, the regular foods he ate could sustain and nourish him, however, when the child became sick, he needed something "extra" to revitalize him. Such is with mankind in general. When people are spiritually "healthy" they can then procure inspiration from the laws of the Torah; however, when mankind is spiritually ill, they need something extra to rejuvenate, and this is the inner treasures of the Torah, the mystical components of the law. As the holy master, the

---

24. Rabbi Sholom Dovber, the fifth Chabad Rebbe, *Safer HaMaamorim*. 5649, -   (New York: Kehot Publication Society, 1986), pp. 259–260.
25. See, Talmud *Megillah* 31a.

Ari Zal (Rabbi Yitzchak Luria, 1534–1572), declared; in this day and age, not only is it permissible, it is actually a mitzvah to teach and reveal the inner parts of the Torah.[26]

This is especially true today, when there is a tremendous hunger for spirituality, a quest to find a deeper explanation to life, and, thereupon, many Jews turn to different sources other than their own (eastern religions, new age movements, and the like). Thus, it is incumbent upon us to speak about those issues whose source is the esoteric, the mystical.

In this book, I will discuss the concept of reincarnation and bring to light that which was spoken about at length in the mystical books of the Kabbalah.[27]

The first kabbalistic book published and made public was the book of "Illumination." In Hebrew, it is known as the Bahir. (The Bahir is also called the "Midrash of Rabbi Nehuniah Ben HaKana" because some Kabbalists attribute the

---

26. Rabbi Hayim Vital Shar Ha'akdamat in the Hakdamah Rabbi Schneur Zalman of Liadi. *Tanya* (New York: Kehot Publication Society, 1965), Igeret Hakodesh 26.

27. Rabbi Naphtali Hirtz Bacharach (seventeenth century) asserts that it is extremely important to write about the issue of reincarnation. See *Emek HaMelech* Hakdamah 2, chapter 2. Albeit that there is a lot of controversy with regards to this text. (See Rabbi Chayim Yoseph Dovid Azulai, *Shem HaGedolim Sefarim Emek HaMelech*.) In an endorsement to its first printing in Amsterdam 1648, the famed Rabbi Yom Tov Lipman Heller (1579–1654) congratulates this book, and writes that it is especially important because it explains the idea of reincarnation.

It is interesting to note that one of the foremost critics of publicizing the idea of reincarnation, Rabbi Levi Ben Yakov Chaviv (1485–1545), writes in his responsa *Ralbach*, chapter 8, that the idea of reincarnation should not be openly discussed, although it can be written about in the printed word. Rabbi Shem Tov Ben Shem Tov (?–1430) calls reincarnation a fundamental belief of Judaism. *Safer Ha'emunot* (Jerusalem: 1969) Shar 7, chapter 4 and chapter 8.

Bahir to this first-century saint and his school of thought.)[28] The Bahir was published in 1176 by the Provence School of Kabbalists.

Approximately one century later, a famed Kabbalist by the name of Rabbi Moshe de Leon published the book of Zohar, "The book of Splendor," which is the compilation of the teachings of Rabbi Shimon Bar Yochai.[29] (Rabbi Shimon Bar Yochai, known as the Rashbi, was a disciple of Rabbi Akiva, although with Rabbi Shimon a new school of thought was developed.) The Talmud[30] tells a story of Rashbi hiding from the Roman officials in a cave. He denounced their ways of governing and was sentenced to death. For 13 years, during his stay in the cave, Rabbi Shimon engaged in all forms of esoteric meditation and prayer until he merited to have the mystical revelation of the prophet Elijah. Thereupon, Elijah taught him the deepest of the world's mysteries, which later on became the main body of the holy Zohar. When Rabbi Shimon left the cave (circa 138 CE), he established his school of mysticism, and some 70 years later, his disciples wrote down his main teachings, forming the holy Zohar. This school

---

28. Rabbi Chayim Yoseph Dovid Azulai, *Shem HaGedolim*. Sefarim Bet 33.
29. See Rabbi Yakov Emdin (1697–1776), *Matpachat Sefarim*, where he writes that the holy Zohar is authentic and most holy for it is the teachings of Rabbi Shimon. Nevertheless, because it wasn't written down and published right away, there are a few verses whose origin is not from Rabbi Shimon. However, it may be noted that many of the examples that he cites as being unauthentic are brought down in Chassidus; for instance, the maxim of the Zohar (see Zohar Mishpatim 23, verse 17), "Whose face is the master of the universe? Rabbi Shimon." See, *Safer HaMaamorim Meluket* (New York: Kehot Publication Society, 1988), vol. 2, p. 301, footnote 7, for the explanation of this verse. See Rabbi Chayim Yoseph Dovid Azulai, *Shem HaGedolim* Sefarim Zayin, 8, for an explanation why Rabbi Yakov Emdin wrote what he wrote.
30. See, Talmud. *Shabbat* 33b.

survived for many years after Rashbi's demise, during which time some minor additions were made.

For more than 1,000 years, these teachings remained mostly in notes. In addition, it was restricted to secret societies of Kabbalists, until it finally came into the hands of a man who was one of the most preeminent mystics of his times, Rabbi Moshe De Leon. He edited and published the Zohar sometime in the 1290s. The first kabbalistic books mentioning the concept of reincarnation are the Bahir[31] and Zohar.[32] The most detailed text written on reincarnation is by the master mystic Rabbi Hayim Vital (1543–1620), who was the prime disciple of preeminent mystic, Rabbi Yitzchak Luria (known as the holy Ari Zal). The book he wrote is titled *Sefer "Shar HaGilgulim"*—the gates of reincarnation. It is from this lofty text that I have based this book.

Begin: *Introduction: Part II*

According to the Bahir, it seems that the concept of reincarnation of the soul is only from one human being who has passed on *into another human being*.

The author of the Bahir offers a parable for the concept of reincarnation:

> There was once a king who had many loyal servants; and being that he admired his servants greatly, he dressed them in the finest clothing possible. It so happens that the servants misbehaved, they dirtied their clothes. The king became very angry with them; he dismissed them and took away their clothing. Then he washed them thoroughly and went to go find some new servants. When he found his new servants, he dressed them with these same (although clean and looking new) clothes. Even though the king does not yet know if these servants will be-

---

31. *Safer HaBahir*, Number 121, 122.
32. See in the Zohar, in numerous places, for instance Parshat Mishpatim, Razin DeGalgultah.

have correctly or not, he nevertheless trusts them that they will be good.[33]

The servants in the parable are human beings who were created to serve God, the Master of the universe. The clothing is an allusion to the soul of man.

The dirtied clothes allude to transgressions. Therefore, it seems suggested from this parable that the soul of man can only be reincarnated—after it undergoes a proper cleansing—into *another servant*, another human being. However, in all other mystical texts and especially in the writings of Rabbi Hayim Vital, they speak overtly of reincarnations of human souls into lower levels of creations, as will be explained in the later chapters.

Rabbi Hayim Vital illustrates in his book[34] that the concept of reincarnation is not only an esoteric teaching whose prime source is the Kabbalah, in the revealed parts of the Torah there are allusions to this theory; for example, when King David says in Psalms, "Please, God, protect my spirit from the sword, and my soul from the dogs."[35] Rabbi Hayim

---

33. *Safer HaBahir* numbers 121, 122. See Talmud. *Shabbat* 152b, the commentary, *MaHarSha*, abbreviation for Morenu HaRav Shmuel Eidels (1555–1631) titled "VeHoyta Nefesh."

34. *Safer Shar HaGilgulim*, Hakdamah 22. See also: Rabbi Menasha Ben Israel, *Nishmat Chayim* (Jerusalem: Yerid HaSefarim, 1995), Maamor 4, chapter 10. The Torah says, "Reuven shall live, and he shall not die." (*Deuteronomy* chapter 33, verse 6.) The *Targum Onkelut* writes: "He shall live now and not experience a second death." According to the Kabbalah this refers to the idea of reincarnation. Reuven should live now and he should not need to come back down here in another reincarnation and then later experience a second death. See, Rabbi Moshe ben Nachman Ramban, *Deuteronomy* chapter 33, verse 6. Rabbeinu Bachya, *Deuteronomy* chapter 33, verse 6. Rabbi Yitzchak of Acco (1250–1340). *Meirat Einayim* (Jerusalem: 1993), Parshat Vezot Habrachah 33–6. See also, Rabbi Menasha Ben Israel, *Nishmat Chayim* Maamor 4, chapter 6.

35. *Psalms*, chapter 22, verse 21.

Vital explains that King David is alluding to the idea of reincarnation. King David is asking God to protect his soul from being reincarnated into a dog. This is the idea of reincarnation from the human species into a lower level of creation, descending into the animal kingdom. Furthermore, according to the teachings of the Holy Ari Zal, there is also the notion of reincarnations of human souls into the level of vegetation and even descending into the level of the inanimate, the inorganic. As the Prophet says, "For a stone from the walls will scream, and a piece of wood from the tree will cry."[36-37] This verse, says Reb Hayim, is also alluding to the concept of reincarnation: a human soul who is now reincarnated into a stone or a piece of wood and is crying from the pain it suffers, that of being a human soul trapped in the body of a stone.

It is self-explanatory that these verses from the revealed scriptures of the Torah are not actual *proof* of reincarnation, rather, they are hints and allusions. In truth, we do not need any proof of reincarnation, from the Niglah of Torah. The very name, Kabbalah, means "receiving,"[38] thus implying

---

36. *Chabakuk*, chapter 2.

37. The Prophet says "Chapeis," which the commentaries say means a piece of wood; see the commentary by Rabbi Shimon Agassi on Shar HaGilgulim. *Benei Aharon*; Talmud. *Chagigah* 16a. *Rashi* titled. "Chapesi."

38. Kabbalah means receiving from a generation previously. See: Rabbi Moshe ben Nachman (1194–1270) *Ramban*, introduction to Torah. *Ramban. Derashas Al Divrei Kohelet.* (Jerusalem: Mossad Harav Kook, 1982), p. 190. Rabbi Joseph Albo (1380–1435) *Safer Haikkarim* Maamor 2, chapter 28. Rabbi Yoseph Ergas (1685–1730) *Shomer Emunim* (Jerusalem: Bepirush U'Beremez, 1965), part 1, number 11. This term Kabbalah is particularly used with regards to mystical thought. See *Rabbeinu Bachya* (1263–1340) *Genesis*. Parshat Vayishlach, chapter 32, verse 10. Rabbi Yoseph Yavatz (1434–1507) on *Avot*, chapter 3, Mishna 12. Rabbi Yoseph Yavatz on *Psalms*, chapter 26, verse 1. Rabbi Eliyahu ben Moshe Di Vidas, *Reshit Chachmah* (Brooklyn: 1984) in the introduction. Rabbi Meir Ben Gabbai (1480–1547). *Avodat Hakodesh* (Jerusalem: Shivilie Orchot

that the Kabbalah was received from one generation to the next, going back until the giving of the Torah on Mount Sinai, some 3,300 years ago at which time God gave and revealed to man the mundane, as well as the mystical, elements of the Torah. And there, God revealed to man all the hidden insights of the Torah including an essential teaching of the Kabbalah, the concept of reincarnation, of which there is no disagreement in terms of its validity in the kabbalistic traditions.[39]

Reincarnation was considered to be a well-established fact throughout our history. Especially in the traditions of the Kabbalah. It was known in all the secret societies to the groups of people who would study the esoteric together. Josephus[40] (the famous Jewish historian, 37–93 CE) writes of an accepted belief by many religious Jews—the concept of reincarnation. To quote, "Do ye not remember at all pure spirits who are in conformity with the divine . . . and in the course of time they are again sent down to inhabit sinless bodies."[41] Moreover, even amongst the gentiles, this concept was well known. Many of the ancient Greek philosophers, who preceded Aristotle, believed in the idea of reincarnation.[42]

HaChaim, 1992), part 2, chapter 13. Rabbi Yoseph Shlomo Delmedigo, known as the Yashar of Candia (1591–1656) *Safer Eilam* (Odessa: 1864), p. 61. This text is brought down by many of the greats of Israel. See Rabbi Yom Tov Lipman Heller, *Tosfot Yom Tov. Berachot*, chapter 1, Mishnah 1. Rabbi Schneur Zalman of Liadi *Sader Hachnasat Shabbat*.

39. Rabbi Joseph Ergas (1685–1730). *Shomer Emunim*, part 1, number 17.

40. See *The Complete Works of Josephus* (Grand Rapids, MI: Kergel Publications, 1981), "Wars of the Jews" book 2, chapter 8, p. 478, 637.

41. *De Bello Judaico*. See Geoffrey Hodson, *Reincarnation Fact or Fallacy* (Wheaton, IL: The Theosophical Publishing House, A Quest Book edition, 1967) p. 17.

42. Rabbi Joseph Ergas, *Shomer Emunim* Part One, Number 37, where he quotes a verse from the holy Zohar. "The Greek philosophy is Pure," which,

For example, the Greek philosopher and mathematician Pythagoras (582–507 BCE) would speak of the previous lives that he led before he descended into the body of Pythagoras.[43] The greatest of the Greek philosophers, Plato (427–347 BCE), writes[44] not only of the concept of reincarnation of souls between one human being and the next, but he also writes of transmigration of souls from humans into the animal kingdom.[45]

---

as explained by Rabbi Menachem Recanti, means that many of the Greek philosophers prior to Aristotle have ideas that are very similar to the Torah's. See also Rabbi Yehudah Halevi (1075–1141) *The Kuzari* (Tel Aviv: Hadron, 1959), Maamor 2, chapter 66. Rabbi Moshe Isserles the Ramah, *Toraht Ha'olah* (Prague: 1570) part 1, chapter 11. Rabbi Aharon Berechyah of Modena (?–1639). *Ma'avar Yavak*. (Vilna: 1880), Maamor 3, chapter 33. Furthermore, many of Aristotle's theories are similar to the Torah's. Legend has it that he received these teachings from Jewish sources. See Rabbi Mayer Eben Aldavia, *Shivilei Emunah*. Nosiv Sheminei (Jerusalem: 1990), p. 352. See Rabbi Menashe Ben Israel, *Nishmat Chayim*, Maamor 4, chapter 21.

43. Rabbi Eliyohu Ben Moshe Vidas, *Reshit Chachmah* Shaar HaYirah. Chapter 13, writes, that Pythagoras believed in reincarnation. See also: Rabbi Eliezer Ezcary, *Safer Cheraidim* (Jerusalem: 1990), chapter 33. Rabbi Menacham Azarya De Fano (1548–1620) *Asarah Maamorot* (Jerusalem: Yismah Lev-Torat Moshe, 1998), Maamor, Olam Katan, chapter 4. Rabbi Yakov Emdin, in *Migdal Oz*. Aliyot HaGilgulim, writes that Pythagoras received these beliefs—reincarnations—from the Early Prophets of Israel. See, Rabbi Menash Ben Isreal, *Nishmat Chayim*. Maamor 4, chapter 21, for a detailed elaboration on this theme. The first to mention the notion that Pythagoras received teachings from Jewish sources is Josephus. See *The Complete Works of Josephus* (Grand Rapids, Michigan: Kergel Publications, 1981). Against Apion, book 1, chapter 22, p. 614.

44. See, Plato, *The Last Days of Socrates*. Phaedo (England: Penguin Books, 1993), p. 14.

45. See, Rabbi Menasha Ben Israel, *Nishmat Chayim*. Maamor 2, chapter 10, where he writes that it was well known—even amongst the writings of the ancient Greeks—that after Jeremiah was exiled to Egypt, he taught Plato the teachings of the Torah. Therefore, many of Plato's teachings coincide with that of the Torah. In fact, there are parallel theories. For every idea that exists in the Torah, there can be found a source in other philosophies. The knowledge of Torah permeates the entire field of knowledge. What is known to the mys-

However, these mystical concepts of Kabbalah were not common knowledge, taught to any student who came to study at the talmudic academies. In fact, the Kabbalah was usually not taught in these academies at all, rather, it was given over from one person to the next, from one generation to the next in secret, studied only in certain secret societies of Kabbalists.[46] Therefore, it is understood that, even amongst many of the great talmudic scholars and rabbis throughout the generations, these teachings were not studied, or even heard of. There were some great Jewish thinkers who claimed that this notion of reincarnation is not a Jewish idea at all. (Even though many of the leaders of Israel did receive this Kabbalah and argued that it is indeed a Jewish concept.[47]) The sages who did not receive this Kabbalah from their teachers argued against reincarnation using logical arguments. But we have already established that the reason we do believe in reincarnation is not because we have found good reason for it, rather, because that is what God revealed to us in the Kabbalah, whose source goes back to Mount Sinai. Hence, any logical argument for or against this concept has no validity, because it is not with our intelligence

---

tics through the Kabbalah was known to the Greeks through philosophy. One is the inner knowledge, while the other is the exterior. See Rabbi Tzadok Hacohen of Lublin (1823–1990). *Likuttei Maamorim*, p. 55.

46. Talmud *Chagigah* 13a. *Pesachim* 119a. See also Talmud *Kedushin* 71a. *Rambam* Hilchot Yesodei Hatorah chapter 2, Halacha 12.

47. See for instance The Bible commentator, *Rabbienu Bachya* (1263–1340) in his commentary to the Bible, Parshat Bechukotai. The illustrious commentator, legalist, and kabbalist, Rabbi Moses Ben Nachman (the Ramban) (1194–1270), in his introduction to the book of Job. The master kabbalist and commentator Rabbi Menachem Recanti (1223–1290), Parshat Shemini. Rabbi Moshe Corodovero (1522–1570) *Pardess Rimonim* (Jerusalem: 1962), Shar 31, chapter 7. By the same author, "Shiur Komah" (Israel: 1966) chapter 4, p. 166.

or our own intuition that we established this belief, it is by revelation.[48]

The philosopher and religious leader, Rabbi Saadiah Gaon (882–942) writes in his monumental philosophical work that there are a few amongst our people who believe in the concept of reincarnation and argue intellectually for this concept.[49] It should be noted that these people believe in this concept of reincarnation *not because they received it* in their Kabbalah (meaning that they were part of the secret society that studied the Kabbalah), but they believe in it for—and through—intellectual reasons alone and on this Rabbi Saadiah argues.

However, had Rabbi Saadiah known of these mystical teachings of the Kabbalah—in our case, the tradition of reincarnation—he would have most definitely agreed with all these teachings.[50] As it is said regarding the great Jewish philosopher and codifier, the Rambam, that toward the end of his life, he found these secret teachings of the Kabbalah, and he declared, had he known before of these teachings, he would have retracted from many of his previous teachings.[51]

---

48. Rabbi Meir Ben Gabbai in *Avodat Hakodesh* (part 2, chapter 32) writes that one cannot intellectually argue against this concept of reincarnation, because it is a tradition that our sages have received from Mount Sinai.

49. *Emunot VeDeyot* (Jerusalem: HaAmnim, 1993), Maamor 6, chapter 8. Rabbi Menasha Ben Israel. *Nishmat Chayim*. Maamor 4, chapter 18.

50. As the philosopher Rabbi Chasdai Cresces (1340–1410) writes in his monumental work, *Or Hashem*. Ma'amor 4. Derush 7. That although intellectually reincarnation does not make any sense, if the belief in reincarnation is an accepted tradition of the Kabbalah he will then accept the concept with certainty. See also, Rabbi Yitzchak Aramah (1420–1494), *Akeidat Yitzchak*. Megilat Ruth. Chapter beginning with the words, "Amar HaMechaber." Where the author explains that although the idea of reincarnation is contrary to rational thought, nonetheless, if this is tradition then he accepts it.

51. Rabbi Dan Yitzchak Abarbanel (1437–1508), *Nachlat Avot* on Avot. At the end of chapter 3. See also, the commentary *Migdal Oz* on the *Rambam*.

There are those who argue in favor of reincarnation, claiming that we must say there are reincarnations, for if there isn't, how can a Just God punish innocent children, children who haven't even had the opportunity to sin, those who, in the words of Talmud, never even "breathed the breath of sin."[52] We encounter young innocent children suffering sicknesses and premature deaths, and there are those who feel compelled to conclude that these children are being punished for what they have done in their previous lives (this argument is one of the more popular arguments for reincarnation, as I will explain in the later chapters of this book). In regards to this reasoning, Rabbi Saadiah argues that there are many answers to this question. For one, we can say that God punishes man in this physical world, in order for man to receive a greater reward in the world to come.[53] Furthermore, he argues, how can reincarnation answer for what happened in the first generations of mankind—when souls descended for the very first time. We must say that in the first generation of people on this earth there were young and innocent people who suffered, and reincarnation would not be a good answer in those scenarios. (Thus, we need the explanation—as he writes earlier—that God punishes man in this world, in order for him to receive a greater good in the world to come.

Hilchot Yesodei Hatorah, chapter 1, Halacha 10. Rabbi Meir Ben Gabbai. *Avodat Hakodesh* part 2, chapter 13. Rabbi Yoseph Ergas. *Shomer Emunim* (Jerusalem: Bepirush U'Beremez, 1965), part 1, number 13. Rabbi Menasha Ben Israel. *Nishmat Chayim*, Maamor 3, chapter 28. *Sader Hadorot*. Rambam. See *Rambam*. Hilchot Yibum VeChelitza, chapter 4, Halacha 6. Where he writes a law, whose source is unknown in our editions of Talmud, and it seems, that the only source for this particular law, is from the Kabbalah, the Zohar.

52. Talmud. *Shabbat* 119b.
53. See Rabbi Saadiah Gaon, *Emunot VeDeyot* (Jerusalem: HaAmnim, 1993), Maamor 5.

This, he writes, is a valid explanation, which can be applicable everywhere and at all times. The suffering of the innocent will be further discussed and argued in Chapter 7.)

Another argument Rabbi Saadiah records (which believers in reincarnation bring as proof for their beliefs) is from the fact that many human beings have character traits and qualities of various animals. For example, people can be passive and submissive like sheep or light and easygoing as birds. From these incidents, they assert that these animalistic attributes come from the soul's previous incarnations, in which the soul was first in the body of sheep or bird, and now reincarnated into a human body. Therefore, these people have these animals' attributes.

Rabbi Saadiah disputes these proofs by saying that this assumption is an oxymoron, because according to them, originally the soul was a human soul, so at first it came down to this world into a human body. After the first body died, the soul was reincarnated into the animal kingdom; for example, into a sheep. When this human soul is in the body of a sheep, they say the body (which is of an animal) affected the soul (the human soul) and transformed the human soul (with its human characteristics) into a soul of an animal (with the attributes of an animal), meaning the body overwhelms soul, matter over spirit. When this soul enters the second human body, they say that the soul (which by now has the traits and character of an animal) affects the human body to act like a animal, to be passive, and the like. According to them, *who eclipses whom*: The body eclipses the soul, or the soul eclipses the body? Furthermore, if what they say is true, then according to them, the soul does not have any firm and true character whatsoever. It does not have an unwavering personality; it is easily changeable (further discussion of reincarnation into animal will be explained in Chapter 5). Consequently Rabbi Saadiah disputes all their proofs.

Over time, there were other Torah sages who, for various reasons, disputed the concept of reincarnation. I will now bring down their arguments; and throughout the book, I will attempt to answer all their questions. Notwithstanding, what was previously mentioned—namely the belief in reincarnation—is not based on intellect but rather, on revelation.

Rabbi Shlomo Ben Aderess (1235–1310) writes in his celebrated responsa that there are a few basic reasons that some people refute reincarnation.[54] One dilemma that arises regarding reincarnation concerns the punishment and reward of the soul. If a soul has multiple incarnations, it is likely that some will be deserving of reward and others of punishment. When the soul is finally elevated and returns to its source, which does it receive? The punishment, or the reward? It seems unfair that the soul which existed within a righteous person would be punished for the deeds of a later incarnation and vice versa.

Another dilemma posed in the responsa (which is also one of the more common confusions regarding reincarnation) concerns the resurrection of the dead. If a soul has multiple incarnations, and each time the body which houses the soul is a completely new person, which of these persons, or bodies, will be the one which resurrects?

---

54. In the question posed to Rabbi Shlomo Ben Aderess, *Teshuvat HaRashba*. Teshuvah 418. See also Rabbi Menasha Ben Israel, *Nishmat Chayim*. Maamor 4, chapter 15. This question was originally posed by Rabbi Yedaya Ha'Penini (?–1305). See: Minchath Kenaoth (Jerusalem: Makor Publishing 1970) by Rabbi Yechiel ben Shmuel of Pisa (c. 1493–c. 1566) for a detailed discussion on the subject.

One of the preeminent Jewish philosophers, Rabbi Joseph Albo (1380–1435), argues against reincarnation in his monumental treatise.[55] According to his philosophy, the purpose of the soul's descent into this physical world is for the soul to experience freedom of choice. The only creation of any world (the physical as well as spiritual worlds) that has the opportunity to choose its own destiny is mankind; therefore, the soul descends into this world. What then is the purpose of reincarnation? The soul's first descent accomplished the experience of freedom of choice. What would the soul gain from another descent? Hasn't the soul already achieved its purpose?

Rabbi Dan Yitzchak Abarbanel (1437–1508) cites a few common arguments against reincarnation,[56] one of which concerns the "shape" of the soul, its own unique form. Each soul has its own "vessel," its particular body into which it fits. How then, can one soul animate different bodies, through multiple incarnations?

Another reason people cite as an argument is that if most people are reincarnated souls, then why don't a substantial number of people remember their previous lives?

These are the most commonly asked questions concerning reincarnation. As we progress in the book, I will endeavor to resolve these difficulties.

---

55. *Safer Haikkarim* (Israel: 1990). Maamor 4, chapter 29.
56. See his commentary on the Bible. *Deuteronomy.* Parshat Teitzei. See also Rabbi Menasha Ben Israel, *Nishmat Chayim*. Maamor 4, chapter 17.

1
The Soul and Its Eternity

Prior to an in-depth analysis of reincarnation, we must address the issue of soul, *what* is being reincarnated. We must first fully comprehend what is the soul—or souls—of man that is reincarnated.

When a person looks at himself and wants to examine himself, he asks, "Who am I?" and "What am I?" The initial and natural instinct is for one to point and look at one's own physical body. However, as one begins contemplating one's physical body, one starts thinking which *part* of the body is the unequivocally real 'me'. If a person were to lose one of his body parts, such as a foot, would that mean he is no longer a complete being? Is he not essentially the same person he was before? In pre-modern times, one might have thought that his body was his real self, and if he does lose an organ he is rendered an incomplete being. However, with the advent of modern medicine, missing organs can be replaced by those belonging to another person. Does that mean that *he* then becomes *the person whose organ he now has*? Today, one can even have a heart transplant and receive another's heart, a vital organ which we think of as being very personal and almost as having its own personality. When the heart which beats inside a person belonged to another at one time, who exactly is this person? Does his heart now define who he is? Is he now another person?

We understand that losing an organ or receiving someone else's organ does not change the essence of who one is. We therefore arrive at the conclusion that the real *you* is something infinitely more complex and ethereal than the physical body. It has been termed, the soul. Each person possesses his own distinct soul, namely, one's memories, personality traits, distinct qualities, and the like. When we speak of soul, it does not mean only one aspect of the soul—one's emotions but not intellect, or one's intellect, and not emotions—we speak of a complete soul, a unique personality with all its complexities, a distinctive way of thinking, feeling, and enjoying life. The totality of one's being.

The first Chabad Rebbe, Rabbi Schneur Zalman of Liadi (1745–1813), was once playing with his grandchild Menachem Mendel (1789–1866). (This child grew up to become one of the Chabad Rebbes, the third in the Chabad dynasty.) Whilst playing with the child, he asked him, "Where is Zeide?" (Zeide is grandfather in the Yiddish dialect.) The child answered him by pointing his finger at his Zeide. The Rebbe asked him, "Where exactly are you pointing your finger? If you are pointing at my feet, you should know that my feet are not Zeide. They are only the feet of Zeide. If you are pointing to my arm, then know that my arms are not Zeide; they are only the arms of Zeide. And if you are pointing to my head, know that it is the head of Zeide but not Zeide. And even if you are pointing to my entire body, you should know that the body is only the body of Zeide. My question is,

'Where is Zeide? Who is the one that tells my feet to start walking, my arms to wave, and my brain to think? Where am I?" After a while, the child left the room. When he reentered the room, he called out loud "Zeide, Zeide," and when his grandfather turned around, he smiled to the boy and said, "*Here is Zeide*. This undivided being is Zeide. The totality of Zeide, is Zeide."

In the history of philosophy, there have been many theories concerning the soul, from the loftiest ideas to the most mundane. When people speak of the soul, they refer to man's predominant character, the compelling force in a human's life, "the real self." The early Greeks, in general (who termed the soul, the 'psyche') and, more specifically, one of the great philosophers in ancient Greece, Anaxagoras (500–428 BCE), believed that 'Nous', reason, intellect, is man's true self. (According to his conviction, the Nous is the controlling and cause of arrangement for the entire universe, not only for man.) Plato—as well as his disciple Aristotle (384–322, BCE), believed that the supreme soul is the human soul, "the rational soul." Plato, in *The Republic*,[1] describes the soul as having three divisions, which he terms: reason, spirit, and appetite. The first; reason, is the awareness of a goal or value. The second soul; spirit, is the drive toward actions. The last; appetite, is the desire to obtain objects for the physical body. However, the essence of the soul is the rational part. Therefore, according to him, the essence of man is his capacity to reason. Man is an *animal rationale*, a knowing animal. This is his predominant being.

Nevertheless, some argue that emotions (feelings) are man's predominant essence. The founder of positive philosophy, who

---

1. *The Republic* (Oxford University Press, 1990), part 2, chapter XIII, p. 129.

later became the founder of the Religion of Humanity; the French philosopher, Auguste Comte (1798–1857) in his revolt against intellect over emotion argues the *supremacy of feelings* of love over pure raw intellect. "Love then, is our principle, Order our basis, and progress our end."[2] Hence, the essence of man is his feelings. The German philosopher Arthur Schopenhauer (1788–1860), argues that neither intellect nor emotions are the predominant force of life, rather, man's subconscious will is his force. Man is a metaphysical animal, a creature to whom will is its force.

In medieval philosophy, there is an argument between the Aristoteliens and the Augustinians regarding which of the two are the essence of soul, intellect or will. Descartes (1596–1650) said that will is supreme. Man may have finite understanding, but infinite will. Others claimed the supremacy of intellect over will. Pascal (1623–1662) says that understanding is through the heart, truth is known through the heart.[3] Therefore, the emotions are supreme. Thus, we find many different theories regarding the soul. According to the view of the Torah, each one of these philosophers is touching a bit of the truth; they are all grasping for the whole truth, but only reaching a part of it. In each one of us, there are actually three souls,[4] three levels of consciousness, each

---

2. See Samuel Enoch Stumpf, *Socrates To Sartre* (New York: McGraw-Hill Book Company, 1996), chapter 16, p. 345.

3. See *Pensées* (London, England: Penguin Books, 1966), Number 110, 292.

4. Jewish philosophy discusses three souls: A) A soul similar to the soul of all vegetative, a soul which propels growth; B) A soul analogous to the animal soul, which causes movement; C) A human intellectual soul. There is an argument if these souls are three distinct souls, or parts of one soul. There are those who say that these souls are distinct, separate entities. See the following sources for the argument of 3 distinct souls: Rabbi Shlomo Eben Gabriel (1021–1069). *Makor Chaim*. Shar 5, chapter 20. Rabbi Avraham Eben Ezra (1089–1164).

level higher than the next. And which of these souls dominates one's existence is decided by the individual. It depends on which spiritual level one has achieved.

The lowest level of soul is the animalistic soul, the soul which animates and gives life to the inanimate body, the soul which transforms a lifeless body into a living organism. This soul is the lifeblood of the body. The Torah states,[5] "For the blood is the Soul." Kabbalah explains this to mean that the soul is in the blood.[6]

During the early periods of the Gaonim (the fifth and sixth centuries CE), the arguments of the Karaites were renewed. The Karaites were a group of Jewish people who did not believe in the oral law, in the oral tradition of the Torah, the Talmud, Midrash, and so on. Being that they did not accept the Rabbinical interpretations, they took many of the bible's metaphors and allusions literally.

Kohelet chapter 7, verse 3. Rabbi Bachya Ibn Pakudah. *Torat HaNefesh*, chapter 4 and chapter 6. The *Rambam*, however, argues that there is only one soul, with three types of manifestations. See *Rambam*. *Shemonah Perakim*, chapter 1. See also Rabbi Mayer Eben Aldavia. *Shivilei Emunah*. Nosiv Shishi (Jerusalem: 1990), p. 294. Rabbi Shimon Ben Tzemach Duran (1361–1444) Magen Avot (1785: Livorno) Part 2, chapter 4, p. 35A. Rabbi Gershon ben Shlomo (13th century) Shar HaShamaim (Israel: 1968), Maamor 11, p. 71. Rabbi Menasha Ben Israel. *Nishmat Chayim*. Maamor 2, chapter 15. Rabbi Moshe Metrani (1500–1580) Beit Elokim (Jerusalem: Otzer Hasefarim, 1985), Shar Hayesodot chapter 62.

They all speak of the intellectual soul being the highest soul. See, however, Rabbi Moshe ben Nachman. *Ramban. Genesis.* Chapter 2, verse 7. *Rabbeinu Bachya. Genesis,* chapter 2, verse 7. Where they equate the highest level of soul, the intellectual soul, with the Godly soul. The Kabbalah speaks of three distinct souls: A) The animal soul, which includes the vegetative; B) The intellectual soul; C) The Godly soul, which is a part of God.

5. *Deuteronomy*, chapter 12, verse 23.

6. See, Rabbi Schneur Zalman of Liadi. *Tanya* (New York: Kehot Publication Society, 1965), chapters 2 and 9.

One of their leaders was a man by the name of Anon.[7] He argued that the abovementioned verse in the Bible means, literally, that the soul of man is his blood. Blood is the soul (as the beliefs of a few of the ancient Greeks, the Stoics, etc.). Rabbi Saadiah Gaon, who was one of the vigorous opponents to their ways of thinking, writes that we find many times in the Torah that it will mention a concept by its location; for instance, the Torah calls speech "the tongue," because the tongue is where the speech is located. Thus Rabbi Saadiah argues that the Torah calls the soul, the blood, because it is in the blood that the soul resides.[8]

This lowest level of soul is called the *Nefesh HaBahamit*, the animalistic soul. The level of this soul is explained as the "physical of the spiritual,"[9] the spiritual that can animate the physical. This soul connects with the spiritual—namely, the most refined aspect—of the physical, which is the blood and, through that, animates the corporeal body. In this state of soul, a human being is likened to an animal, because everything he desires and all he does is only for personal gain, and for his own personal survival.

Everything in the spiritual dimensions has a division of ten.[10] The soul too, contains ten states of conscious-

---

7. See Isaac Hirsh Weise, *Dor Dor VeDorshav* (Jerusalem: Ziv Publication, 1960), Vol. 4, p. 41.

8. Rabbi Saadiah Gaon, *Emunot VeDeyot* (Jerusalem: Haamnim, 1993). Maamor 6, chapter 1.

9. See, Rabbi Yehudah HaLevi (1075–1141), *The Kuzari* (Tel Aviv: Hadran, 1959). Maamor 4, chapter 26. See Rabbi Yoseph Yitzchak, the sixth Chabad Rebbe. *Safer HaMaamorim 5708* (New York: Kehot Publication Society, 1986), p. 23.

10. Ten being the number of completion. See: Rabbi Meir Ben Gabbai, *Avodot Hakodesh* (Jerusalem: Shevilei Orchot HaChaim, 1992) Part 1, chapter 14, and *Derech Emunah* (New York: Kehot Publication Society, 1987), response 3. Rabbi Moshe Cordovero, *Pardess Rimonim* (Jerusalem: 1962), Shar 2. Rabbi

ness,[11] corresponding to the ten heavenly *Sefirot* (through these *Sefirot*, God sustains all the worlds). These ten are further subdivided into three compartments: intellect, emotion, and action.

The first three are intellect: *Chochmah*, wisdom—intuitive thoughts; *binah*, understanding—comprehension; and *da'at*, knowledge—internalizing the thoughts. The next three are the attributes of emotions: *chesed*, kindness—benevolence; *gevurah*, might—power, prevalence; and *tiferet*, beauty—compassion which is a synthesis of the first two emotional attributes. The next three are the attributes of action, actions which stem from the intellect or the emotions: *netzach*, endurance—victory, for a person to overcome all obstacles in their paths, to persevere and follow through; *hod*, splendor—submitting, humbling one's self to overcome. Going under the problem instead of over,[12] *Yesod*; the connection and the foundation between one's self and what one is going to do; *Malchut*, kingship or sovereignty, stands separate from the previous nine. For *Malchut* is a state of being, rather than an activity. It is an awareness of royalty. Thus, all the actions are manifested in a glorious way. In the animalistic soul, whose primary goal and ambition is to sustain its own existence, the essence of the soul is the *emotions*. It is only concerned with how it will feel and how it will be affected. Everything revolves around one's own subjective feelings. Thus, the essence of

---

Joseph Ergas, *Shomer Emunim* (Jerusalem: Bepirush: Bepirush U'Beremez, 1965), Part 1, number 51.

11. Rabbi Schneur Zalman of Liadi, *Tanya* (New York: Kehot Publication Society, 1965), chapter 6.

12. Rabbi Schneur Zalman of Liadi, *Likutei Torah* (New York: Kehot Publication Society, 1996), Parshat. Massei, p. 90.

this soul is emotion; and, therefore, the purpose of the intellect in this soul is only to serve the emotions. One uses the intellect to find and create new ways for one to acquire pleasure.

Although in the Talmud[13] this animalistic soul is called the "evil inclination," *Yetzer Ha-Ra*, the truth is that it is not actually a bad inclination. By its very nature, it is an inclination that wants to sustain and perhaps give pleasure to its own existence. It is what we call "survival instincts."

The Midrash[14] says on the verse in Genesis,[15] "And lo it was good." That this refers to the good inclination. "And lo it was *very good*" refers to the evil inclination. The question asked is as follows; why is the evil inclination *very good*? The Midrash answers, were it not for the evil inclination, no one would build a home, marry, have children, or do business. From here, we see clearly what the role of this inclination is. It is not evil, as in a harmful instinct, rather evil, meaning egotistic and selfish. For if man did not care for himself, he would not function as a healthy member of society. Although these essential motions are things that a person is obligated to do according to the Torah, being that they are done by most, purely for personal gain, they are termed evil. (Although selfishness in and of itself is not necessarily evil, selfishness can lead man to evil.)[16]

Surpassing this animalistic level of soul, one reaches a higher realm of soul—the part of soul that is called the *Nefesh*

---

13. See for instance, Talmud. *Sukah* 52b, *Berachot* 61a.
14. *Midrash Rabbah Genesis* Parsha 9, chapter 7.
15. *Genesis*, chapter 1, verse 31.
16. Hence, the Midrash says: It is man that makes the *Yetzer HaRa*, evil. See *Midrash Tanchumah* Bereishit, chapter 7.

HaSechely, "the intellectual soul." This is the level of pure intellect. This soul is the intellectual soul yet it contains all ten sefirot, including emotions and emotions of actions. In this level of soul, the intellect is not the way it is in the animal soul, whence the intellect is dictated by the emotions. Conversely, these emotions are dictated by the intellect. The emotions one experiences are directly channeled from the intellect. These emotions are termed in the kabbalah, "*Yinikah*,"[17] milking, absorbing. One's emotions on this level of soul are nourished by the intellect.

Pure intellect is the capacity to rise above oneself, to transcend one's own personal feelings, and to act in the way one's objective intellect advises. This power is what is called "freedom of choice." Which means that, even if, by natural instinct one might be inclined to act in a certain manner, for that is the emotional reaction one feels most immediately comfortable with, nevertheless, with the power of one's intellect, one can rise above the situation and dictate the emotions. (A person can—if he so desires—choose his own destiny simply by allowing the intellect to dictate the emotions rather than the other way around.) This intellectual level of soul is what the Rambam[18] calls the *Tzurah*.

The loftiest level of soul is the Godly soul, the *Nefesh Elokit*. For one to attain this level of soul, one must reach the age of physical maturity, in addition to mental and spiritual maturation.[19] When we speak of Godliness in general, and specifi-

---

17. Rabbi Shalom Dovber, Fifth Chabad Rebbe, *Safer HaMaamorim 5670* (New York: Kehot Publication Society, 1984), p. 132.
18. See *Hilchot Yesodei HaTorah*, chapter 4, Halacha 8, 9. *Hilchot Tishuvah*, chapter 8, Halacha 3.
19. Although the soul generally enters the body at conception. (See, Talmud *Sanhedrin*, 91b.) It does not permeate the body until birth. (See Rabbi

cally, the Godly soul, we are actually speaking of selflessness. When we say a person is in touch with his Godly soul, we are saying that he acts selflessly. When someone does another person a favor, for instance, one gives charity to a poor man, it is possible that his motives are either selfish or a selfless. One can give the charity for a selfish reason—it makes him feel good to give to someone else who is less fortunate. If not for his benevolence, this poor man might starve. Hence, every time he gives charity, it only serves to boost his ego. The more he gives, the more he *is*. Or conversely, a person can give charity because he actually feels the other person's pain. The charitable act is done entirely out of empathy for the person in need. Consequently, when we speak of "a Godly person," someone who is in touch with his Godly soul, we mean to say someone who does good, not so that he should feel good, but because he feels the other person's pain.

Furthermore, a truly Godly person[20] carries out all the Divine commandments solely by virtue of them being commandments. He does it because it is what God wants from him. His motives are entirely selfless, above even the desire to become more holy or connected with God, he fulfills God's desires solely to serve his master.

Yehudah Loew, *Nesivat Olam* (Israel: 1980), Nesiv HaTzdaka, chapter 3.) And it completely permeates the body, at maturity. See: *Shulchan Aruch HaRav*, in the beginning (second edition) chapter 4; Rabbi M. M. Schneerson. *Likutie Sichot* (New York: Kehot Publication Society, 1964), vol. 3, p. 763. Vol. 10, p. 45. See also: Rabbi Pinchas Eliyahu Ben Meir of Vilna (1743–1821), *Safer Habrit* (Jerusalem: Yerid HaSefarim, 1990), Part 2, Maamor 1, chapter 3. (See however *Midrash Kohelet*, Parsha 4:13.)

20. Rabbi Schneur Zalman of Liadi, *Tanya* (New York: Kehot Publication Society, 1965), chapter 10.

The Godly soul is divided into five comparments.[21] (In addition to the division of the soul into ten *Sefirot*.[22]) The highest level of this soul is called *Yichidah*, desire. A lower level is called *Cha-yah*, will. Lower than that is *Neshamah*, intellect, and then *Ruach*, emotions. The lowest is called *Nefesh*, spirit of actions. This division of five corresponds to the four general spiritual worlds and the level above them, which is the level of Keter. The explanation of this in brief is as follows. Before God created all the worlds, there was only the *Ein Sof*, "the infinite light of God." Thus, when God (the infinite) decided to create these worlds (the finite), He created it through a process which the Kabbalah calls *Tzimtzumim*, constrictions. Namely, a process of progressive dimming, occultations, and condensations of the infinite light, the *Ein Sof*—finally, revealing levels of finite. This brought about numerous levels of worlds, one lower than the next.

These levels are divided into five comprehensive categories, Keter and the four worlds. The highest, Keter, is also known as "Adam Kadmon," the primordial man. This is an anthropomorphic term; thus, Kadmon denotes being primary of all primaries. This level is also called "Keter Elyon," the higher crown.

---

21. *Midrash. Bereishit Rabbah* Parshah 14, chapter 9. *Midrash Rabbah. Deuteronomy*, Parsha 2, chapter 37. See also Talmud *Berachot*, 10a. Rabbi Saadiah Gaon, *Emunot VeDeyot* (Jerusalem: Haamnim, 1993), Maamor 6, chapter 3. According to the Talmud and Midrash, these five names are five expressions of the same concept. However, the Kabbalah explains these five names, as five separate levels of soul, five distinct states of consciousness.

22. The animalistic soul, which we previously divided into three categories, does not embody the fifth level of *Yichidah*. Because the concept of *Yichidah* means total nullification, which in the animal soul would translate, total self-nullification to the physical necessities of man. Such a lowly level of soul does not exist in man. (The Talmud alludes to this, when it says, "A demon does not possess a shadow of their shadow." Talmud, *Yivomot* 122.)

The first of the four worlds is called "Atzilut," world of emanation. Then came "Beriah," the world of creation. Following that is "Yetzirah," the world of formation. And finally the world of "Asiyah," the world of action or completion. Although all of the ten *Sefirot* emanate and function in every one of these worlds, nevertheless, in each one of these worlds in particular, specific *Sefirot* dominate.

In the lowest of spiritual worlds, the world of *Asiyah*, action, the predominant features are from the lower levels of the ten *Sefirot*, the *Sefirot* of actions, the spirit behind the actions. (We speak here not of action itself, rather, the spirit of the action, for the worlds we speak of are in the spiritual realm.) Accordingly, the world of Asiyah is analogous to the spirit compelling the action. That which causes one to do an action with Godly intent.

The world above Asiyah is the world of *Yetzirah*, formation. In this world the higher levels of the *Sefirot*, those of emotion, dominate. (This is a world of angels, serving their creator with a submission borne of pure and unadulterated emotion.[23]) Correspondent to this world is *Ruach*, the level of soul which determines one's emotional attachment to God.

A higher level of world, and thus a deeper dimension in soul, is the world of *Beriah*, creation. This is the world of in-intellect, whence the most elevated of the ten *Sefirot*, the intellectual *Sefirot*, dominate. In the world of *Beriah*, the angels serve God through intellect.[24] Thus, in man, this world corresponds to his level of *Neshamah*, intellect.

---

23. See Rabbi Schneur Zalman of Liadi. *Tanya* (New York: Kehot Publication Society, 1965), chapter 39. Thus, angels are likened to animals. (See in the beginning of the Prophecy of Ezekiel, because they both act according to their emotions and instincts.)

24. Rabbi Schneur Zalman of Liadi, *Likutie Torah* (New York: Kehot Publication Society, 1996), Parshat Emor, p. 32b.

Surpassing this level of intellect, we arrive at the level of *Cha-Yah*, Will. This correlates to the world of *Atzilut*, emanation, a world that, in a sense, *is above creation*. As explained in Kabbalah,[25] the word *Atzilut* is derived from the Hebrew word *Eitzel*, which means close, denoting the close proximity—almost to the level of unity—between this world and its source, its creator. Translating this level of world into the soul of man; the world of *Atzilut* represents a state in which one's entire being is completely permeated with Godliness. One becomes as the world of *Atzilut*, one with the creator. One's will and quintessential being, loses itself in Godliness.

The loftiest state of soul correspondant to the highest level of worlds, that of *Adam Kadmon* (or the level of *Keter*, desire), is the state of *Yichidah*, oneness. This is the level of soul in which we unite with God, so thoroughly and completely, until we cannot even say that there is an existence that is united with God. It is as if it was one to begin with. All the above levels are contained in each and every individual being.[26] Most people may go through their entire lives and never come in contact with the higher reaches of their soul, especially that of *Yichidah*, the great unity. Only

---

25. Rabbi Moshe Cordovero, *Pardess Rimonim* (Jerusalem: 1962), Shar 16, chapter 1. Rabbi Meir Ben Gabbai, *Avodat Hakodesh* (Jerusalem: Shivilie Orchot HaChaim, 1992), part 1, chapter 14.

26. In Chassidus and Kabbalah, it speaks often and clearly regarding souls whose source is from the world of *Atzilut* and those which stem from lower worlds, which seems to imply that not all souls come from, and therefore contain within them, these higher levels. However, as explained in *Safer Shar HaGilgulim*, Hakdamah 2, each individual human being has all levels contained within their soul. The issue in question is only, which of these levels predominates. If the level of *Asiyah* overwhelms the level of *Atzilut*, then we call this person's soul, a soul of *Asiyah*. Conversely, if the level of *Atzilut* predominates, then we call his soul a soul of *Atzilut*. See also Rabbi Schneur Zalman of Liadi, *Tanya* (New York: Kehot Publication Society, 1965), chapter 18.

Tzadikim, or perhaps ordinary people in a moment of truth, merit to touch upon this exalted state of soul. As the first Chabad Rebbe writes,[27] when we come upon ordinary people experiencing moments of intense spiritual feelings, a sudden awakening of exceptional devotion, the reason for this phenomenon may be, that there is a unique and remarkable level in the person's soul: that of *Yichidah*, which can reveal itself at any moment, especially at a time of challenge. Therefore, says the Rebbe, we notice that throughout history, there were many occasions whence non-practicing Jews who were forced to either denounce God or face death willingly went to their deaths, notwithstanding the fact that until then, throughout their entire lives, they had no connection and interest in Godliness. Yet at a moment of truth, they chose God, something that is beyond their comprehension, because the level of *Yichidah* is a connection that goes beyond all rationale, a state of soul that is above and beyond any explanation, above any rational understanding.[28] Therefore, when a person does such an exceptional act of self-sacrifice, we know it comes from a level of soul that is above even his own intellect, above and beyond everything he did or felt until then—the level of *Yichidah*.

In order to fully comprehend the soul and its incarnations, one must be familiar with the inner workings of the

---

27. See Rabbi Schneur Zalman of Liadi, *Tanya* (New York: Kehot Publication Society, 1965), chapter 19. See also Rabbi Menasha Ben Israel, *Nishmat Chayim*, Maamor 4. At the end of chapter 2. Rabbi Nachman of Breslov (1772–1810) *Likutei Moharan* (Jerusalem: Torat HaNetzach, 1997), part 1, chapter 80.

28. See Rudolf Otto, *The Idea of the Holy* (London: Oxford University Press, 1958), chapter titled, "Spirit and Soul as Numinous Entities," where he writes that the divine soul does not merely consist of man being rational, moral, rather primarily that in the depths of man, there is a divine consciousness.

soul as well as its immortality. Immortality can be achieved on various levels.[29] The lowest state of immortality is to experience eternity through other people. For example, if after one's passing, there are other people who give charity in the deceased's name, or otherwise pay tribute to his memory, then the memory of the deceased lives on as long as the other people remember him.[30]

A more exalted state of immortality is the attainment of eternity through one's own actions. If one can accomplish something during a lifetime that will remain in existence forever, then through that action one will also live forever.[31] As the Talmud states in regard to Moses and David,[32] "The works of Moses and David are Eternal." It was Moses who constructed the Tabernacle in the desert, and King David who built the doors for the holy Temple, and both of these constructions are still in existence (although they are now concealed from the human eye). Therefore, we say it is as if they are both still alive because they live on forever through their actions.

Still a greater state of immortality can be achieved through the continuance of one's teachings. When people study one's teachings after one's demise, and his followers continue in his footsteps, the person continues to live. As the

---

29. See Rabbi Meir Ben Gabbai (1480–1547), *Avodat Hakodesh*, Hakdamat Hame chaber.

30. As the custom is for other people to build a mausoleum in honor of the deceased. See The Jerusalem Talmud. *Shekalim* chapter 2, Halachah 5. Or study in his honor. See Talmud. *Yevamot* 122a. *Rashi*. Titled. "Telasa Riglie." See also *Rabbeinu Bachya*. *Deuteronomy* chapter 21, verse 8, with regards to charity.

31. See Rabbi Menasha Ben Israel, *Nishmat Chayim*. Maamor 4, chapter 3.

32. Talmud. *Sotah* 9a.

Talmud states,[33] "A learned person's words of wisdom are his memory." Therefore, the Talmud concludes that there is no reason for us to build a mausoleum when a learned person dies; his teachings themselves are his monument.

Above all the previous states of immortality is the level of eternity. Through one's own children, one may continue living. The Talmud declares,[34] "Yakov (the patriarch Jacob) lives on, his children are alive therefore he is also considered alive." This concept is especially true when one's offspring follow in the direction of his ancestors. If they continue to behave the way the deceased did, they continue his legacy. The Talmud says,[35] "King David had an heir equal to himself, therefore it does not say in the Bible the word 'death' in reference to David."

However, true immortality is attained only through the eternity of the actual physical body. This is the concept of resurrection of the dead. The Midrash states,[36] "There is a small bone in the body, the *Luz*, which never disintegrates, and from this bone, the entire body will be resurrected." When the prophet Isaiah speaks of the resurrection, he says,[37] "God will *revive* the dead." He does not say that God will rebuild the body and will then create a new body, rather, God will *revive* the body, meaning that there are still rem-

---

33. The Jerusalem Talmud. *Shekalim*, chapter 2, Halacha 5.
34. See Talmud. *Tannit* 5b. The philosopher Arthur Schopenhaur argues that man's will to exist eternally causes him subconsciously to go about having children. See also: Rabbi Yehudah ben Yitzchak Abarbanel (?–1535) *Vikuach Al Ahavah* (Israel: 1968), p. 5b.
35. Talmud *Bava Batra* 116a.
36. *Midrash Rabbah Genesis*. Parsha 28, chapter 3. *Midrash Rabbah. Leviticus*. Parsha 18, chapter 1. See also Talmud. *Bava Kamma*. 16b. *Tosfot*. Vehu. Ad loc. Talmud. *Sanhedrin* 92b, the commentary *Maharsha*. Shechipa. Ad loc.
37. See *Isaiah* chapter 26, verse 19.

nants of the body which have not disappeared. From this minute bone (it may be the size of an atom or even smaller), God will resurrect the entire body. Hence, this small Luz bone is the immortality of the physical body.[38]

Furthermore, it is stated, that many righteous people can achieve immortality through their entire physical body.[39] The Talmud says, [40] "Moses did not pass away." The commentaries explain[41] that this means that his physical body did not disintegrate. On the verse, "His [Moses'] eyes did not falter, and his strength did not leave him,"[42] Rashi (Rabbi Shlomo Yitzhaki, 1040–1105) explains that this verse alludes also to the time after Moses' death, for his eyes did not falter nor did his strength leave him even after his demise. It is also feasible (as the great moralist and mystic, Rabbi Judah HaChassid [1150–1217] writes),[43] that God will miraculously sustain the body of a wicked person for a longer period of

---

38. See *Zohar*, part 1. 137a. *Zohar* part 2. p. 28b. See Rabbi M. M. Schneerson, *Likutei Sichot* (New York: Kehot Publication Society, 1972), vol. 6, p. 81. The reward the physical body receives for doing *mitzvot* in this world will be received at the time of the resurrection of the body. Thus, the body cannot dissolve totally after its death, for if it did, the body that will be resurrected will not be the same body that did the *mitzvot*. However, if there remains of the body even one small bone, and God resurrects the body from that bone, then the body receives its rewards.

39. Rabbi Menachem Azaryah De Fano (1548–1620), *Asarah Maamorot*. Maamor Olam Katan (Jerusalem: Yismah Lev-Torat Moshe, 1998), chapter 4. Rabbi Eliyahu ben Moshe Di Vidas. *Reshit Chachmah* (Brooklyn: 1984). Shar Hayirah, chapter 11.

40. See Talmud. *Sotah* 13b. See *Zohar*, part 1, p. 37b.

41. *Eiyun Yakov*. Talmud *Sotah* 13b. Rabbi Yonayhan Eibeschuretz Yarot D'Vosh (Jerusalem: Levin-Epstain) part 1, p. 8b.

42. *Rashi, Deuteronomy*, chapter 34, verse 7. See Talmud. *Tannit* 5b, *Rashi*. Titled. "Af Hu." They—the Egyptians—thought he—Jacob—died; however, in truth he was still alive.

43. *Safer Chassidim* (Jerusalem: Mochon Reshonim), chapter 1143.

time than is normal, in order for his body to have its appropriate refinements (punishments), the punishment being the pain he suffers being decomposed. He explains elsewhere[44] that it is not that the dead body actually feels any of the physical punishment that it receives, for they are done to the lifeless body, rather, the punishment is a psychological anguish which *the soul suffers* on seeing its earthly form being punished and demoralized by decomposition.

Until this point we have discussed the immortality of the physical person. Now I will expound on the immortality of the soul. As mentioned before, there are actually three souls. The purpose of the lowest soul, the animalistic soul, is to give life to the inanimate body, to animate the body. The animalistic soul is the life force of most people, for most people exist in a state of consciousness whence life revolves around one's animalistic needs, such as eating, sleeping, and so on. However, there are more intellectual individuals, who are referred to as the "pursuers of knowledge." They are on a different state of consciousness and are animated by their intellectual soul. And still higher, there exist men on the loftiest spiritual level attainable by humans, these are "the righteous men." Their state of consciousness is such that their Godly soul is what animates them, keeping them alive. These three levels of soul; the animalistic, the intellectual, and finally, the Godly comprise the "ladder of perfection," a system of elevating oneself, for which all humanity must strive. The higher one climbs, the greater level of soul is revealed. Each level of soul represents a state of consciousness. The higher the soul, the higher the state of consciousness.

---

44. See Ibid. chapter 1163. See also Rabbi Saadiah Gaon, *Emunot VeDeyot*, Maamor 6, chapter 7.

The Rambam calls the animalistic soul "the *soul* which *needs the body*,"[45] meaning that the soul has but one purpose and one reason that it was created: that it should animate the physical body. Therefore, when the body expires and does not continue to function as a living organism, this animating soul has no reason to exist. From this he concludes that when the body dies, so does its soul, because this soul was created only to suit this specific body.

From the Rambam, it seems suggested that the soul was created immediately preceding the creation of the body. It has *no prior existence*. However, from the Kabbalah,[46] it seems to be understood that the animalistic soul has a preexistence going back to the beginning of creation. This was a time when God created all souls, the Godly as well as the animalistic. (Reconciling the Rambam's view with that of the Kabbalah, it is explained that although individual souls are created specifically for "their" particular body, they are all taken from one general, "generic" soul which was created in the beginning of time.)[47]

The animalistic soul (as well as the intellectual and Godly souls) has within itself two divisions.[48] One is called the *Nefesh Ha-Mekayem*, the soul that sustains the body, giving it its very existence. This is the part of the soul which re-

---

45. See *Hilchot Yesodei HaTorah*, chapter 4, Halacha 9.
46. *Safer Shar HaGilgulim*, Hakdamah, 23. Rabbi Dan Yitzchak Abarbanel writes that when the Midrash states, that on the sixth day of creation God created the souls of man. (See *Midrash Rabbah. Genesis*. Parsha 7, chapter 5.) The soul the Midrash is referring to is the animating soul; the lower levels of soul. See *Mifalot Elokim* (Jerusalem: Otzer Hapaskim, 1993), Maamor 8, chapter 6.
47. See Rabbi Shemuel, the fourth Chabad Rebbe. *Igrois Koidesh, Admur Moharash* (New York: Kehot Publication Society, 1993), pp. 94, 95.
48. Rabbi Yoseph Yitzchak, the sixth Chabad Rebbe. *Safer HaMaamorim 5694* (New York: Kehot Publication Society, 1962). Ki Cheilek, p. 29.

sides within every single creation, from the greatest of men to the humblest of stones. It is a spiritual soul, which gives form to creation; without this soul there can be no existence. The second division of the soul is called the *Nefesh Ha-Mechaya*, the soul that gives the body its life, vitality, and animation—"the life soul." When a person passes on, his soul departs his body. Yet, the body continues to retain its form even after the soul's passing. How is this possible if the soul which keeps the body in existence has departed? We maintain that only the soul that gives the body its life and vitality departs. Only the *Nefesh Ha-Mechayah* leaves the body. The body does not instantly dissolve into nothingness, because the soul that gives the body its existence still permeates the entire body. This *Nefesh Ha-Mekoyem* (that which resides within the lifeless body) has throughout the person's life received its energy from the *Nefesh Hamechayeh*, the life-giving soul. After the person's passing, there still remains within him what the Kabbalah calls a "*Kistah*" of life, a small quantity of life.[49] This life energy is enough to give the *Nefesh Hamekayem* the vitality necessary to maintain the body's existence, although this small "*Kistah*" does not last long. As it leaves the body over time, the body disintegrates.[50]

What we see from the above is that the animalistic soul does not live forever; it is mortal, when its vessel, the body

---

49. *Kistah* is a small measurement. Talmud. *Avodah Zarah* 34b, *Rashi*, *Kistah*.

50. However, there is a difference between the first few days following one's death and the next few days. See: Jerusalem Talmud. *Moed Katan* chapter 3, Halacha 5. See Rabbi Nison Ben Reuvain (1290–1380), *Derashot HaRan*, Derush 7.

dies, so does the soul.[51] However, it should be noted that when we speak of the Jewish soul, even the animalistic part of it does experience some form of immortality, for after the body's demise, the animalistic soul of a Jew transforms and becomes a "Throne for Holiness."[52] Nevertheless, this is not considered real immortality, because its eternity differs from its existence in the body. In the body, it was an animalistic soul; now, in its afterlife, it metamorphosed into a holy existence. The definition of eternity is to exist *in the same state* forever.

The higher soul, the intellectual soul, which the Rambam calls the *Tzurah*, does have immortality. As the Rambam writes, "when the *individual* body will disintegrate . . . this soul will not decay. . . . It will understand and comprehend thoughts, loftier thoughts which are above any tangible thoughts. It will know its creator and it will endure forever and ever."[53]

According to the Rambam, the ultimate reward that man can receive, the reward of which the prophet says, "No eye has seen other than God,"[54] is when the soul exists on its own without the body.[55] Hence, according to the Rambam, even after the time of the resurrection, there will be a time of death, and only then will the soul—separately—receive these ulti-

---

51. See *Rambam*. Hilchot Yesodei Hatorah, chapter 4, Halacha 9. *Hilchot Teshuvah*, chapter 8, Halacha 3. See also *Orchot Tzadikim*. (Author unknown. Many believe it to be written circa eight hundred years ago.) Shar Yirat Shamayim (Jerusalem: Orot Chaim, 1986), p. 275.

52. Rabbi Schneur Zalman of Liadi, *Likutei Torah* (New York: Kehot Publication Society, 1996), Parshat, Shelach, p. 40.

53. *Hilchot Yesodei HaTorah*, chapter 4, Halacha 9. See *The Guide to the Perplexed* (Jerusalem: Mossad Harav Kook, 1977), part 1, chapter 41. Part 2, chapter 27.

54. *Isaiah*, chapter 64, verse 3. See Talmud. *Berachot* 34b.

55. *Hilchot Teshuvah*, chapter 8, Halachah 7.

mate rewards. However, most Kabbalists maintain that the ultimate reward for the soul, is when it is resurrected in the body, when the soul is joined once again with the body.[56]

The world that the soul inhabits after death, is known as *Gan Eden,* Paradise. Some Kabbalists refer to it as the world of souls.[57] In the Kabbalah,[58] this world is said to exist in the *Sefira of Binah*, the *Sefira* of Comprehension. *Gan Eden* is a world in which "the *Ein Sof* is revealed. The Infinitude of Godliness in the appearance of Finite. And in this state, it is possible for the soul to comprehend Godliness and thus, receive pleasure from the Infinite Light."[59] Hence, the Talmud says,[60] "Honorable is the man who enters to this world—Gan Eden—with the Talmud in his possession." The studying of the Talmud in this world allows one to fully comprehend the Torah, with its true mystical and inner meanings in the world of *Gan Eden*.

The Rambam's theory on immortality seems to be quite similar to the theory of immortality by Plato. According to Plato's theory, when the soul leaves the body, it leaves its prison. "Now surely the soul can reason best, when it is free of all distractions, such as hearing or sight or pain or pleasure of any kind—that is when it leaves the body to its own devices."[61]

---

56. See Ramban, *Torah's Ha-Adam*, Sharr HaGmul, toward the end.
57. Rabbeinu Bachya, *Kad HaKemach* (Jerusalem: Mossad Harav Kook, 1995), Hasgacha, p. 139. See Rabbi Moshe Chayim Luzzatto (1707–1747). *Derech HaShem*, part 1, chapter 3.
58. The Master Kabbalist Rabbi Yoseph Gikatalia (1248–1323), *Shaarey Orah*, Shar 8. See also *Pardess Rimonim*, 8:9, 23:3. *Likutei Torah*, 4:88. Chesed le'Avraham (Jerusalem: Yerid HaSefarim), part 5, chapter 52.
59. Rabbi Schneur Zalman of Liadi. *Likutei Torah* (New York: Kehot Publication Society, 1996), Parshat Tzav, p. 11.
60. See in numerous places in the Talmud, for instance, *Pesachim* 50a.
61. See *The Last Days of Socrates* (London: Penguin Books, 1993). The Phaedo, p. 118.

However, according to Plato, this form of immortality for the soul is experienced only by the philosophers, ones who pursued knowledge during their lifetimes. As he writes in the name of his teacher Socrates, "But no soul which has not practiced philosophy, and is not absolutely pure when it leaves the body, may attain to the divine nature; that is only for the lover of learning."[62] However, according to the Torah view, "Every single Jew has a portion in the world to come (Gan Eden)."[63] Even the most simple of men have a share in that world. Everyone enters *Gan Eden*, not only the philosophers. (Furthermore, even sinners will merit entry to Gan Eden after a period of 12 months of punishment.[64]) This is the immortality of one's intellectual soul, which, even after the passing of one's physical body and "life sustaining" soul, lives on in Paradise until the time of the resurrection of the dead, when it will return to its physical body.

When speaking of reincarnation, the soul we speak of is the Godly soul. It is this soul which reincarnates, and which we will discuss in the following chapters. This is the soul that is "Truly, a part of God above."[65] It is self-evident that this soul is infinite and everlasting and ultimately immortal. It existed before the creation of the body and will exist well after the body disintegrates. In the following chapters, we will analyze its eternity. How and where does this soul exist?

---

62. See Ibid, p. 141.
63. See Rambam. *Hilchot Teshuvah*, chapter 3, Halacha 5. See Mishnah, *Sanhedrin*, chapter 10, Mishnah 1.
64. See Mishnah, *Eduyot*, chapter 2, Mishnah 10.
65. See *Job*, chapter 31, verse 2. See *Ramban on Torah*, Genesis, chapter 2, verse 7. See Rabbi Schneur Zalman of Liadi. *Tanya* (New York: Kehot Publication Society, 1965), chapter 2. See chapter 3, footnote 11.

2
The Purpose of the Soul's Descent

Before the Godly soul descended to this physical world to inhabit a corporeal body it existed in the most holy and lofty state conceivable. Yet, it leaves its state of pure holiness and becomes a part of a coarse, material existence. Why did this lofty being descend so low? Why did it come down to this inferior world? Some answer, that the soul descends for the purpose of reaching higher spiritual levels, but this answer does not suffice, because even the highest levels that it will attain in this physical world will never equal the level of *Davakus*—oneness, unity—that it experienced in the upper worlds prior to its descent below. As the *Tanya* states,[1] "For even if one is a perfectly righteous person, serving God with fear and great love, he can not attain the degree of attachment to God, as it had before it came down to this lowly

---

1. See Rabbi Schneur Zalman of Liadi, *Tanya* (New York: Kehot Publication Society, 1965), chapter 37.

world. Not a fraction of it, and there is no comparison or similarity between them at all as is clear to every understanding person."

The reason these levels cannot be attained in this world is that, being that the soul resides within a physical body and universe, it is obstructed and confined by the physicality.

Thus, it is explained that the purpose of the soul's descent is not for its personal gain or achievement, rather, to refine and elevate the physical body, and, in extension, the entire physical world.[2]

The ultimate purpose of creation is to draw down Godliness to dwell in and permeate this physical world.[3] In the words of the Midrash,[4] "To create a dwelling place for God on this world." And the reason for this is because God desired[5] to inhabit and permeate, not only the spiritual worlds above, but this mundane and material world as well. And in doing so, making this world a Godly world. We can reach this objective by undoing (so to speak) what God has done. God created this physical world out of nothingness, *Ex Nihilo*,

---

2. Rabbi Avraham Azulay, *Chesed LeAvraham*, part 4, chapter 4.

3. See Rabbi M. M. Schneerson, *Likutie Sichot* (New York: Kehot Publication Society, 1972), vol. 6. Parshat Shemot, 2 p. 21, Where it is explained that, according to all the reasons, which are stated in the Kabbalah as the purpose for creation. For instance, for humans—independent un-Godly creatures—to serve him. [See *Zohar Parshat Bo*, 44:2.] So man shall recognize his greatness. [See *Aietz Chayim*, Sharr Hakelalim in the beginning.] All agree that the ultimate purpose for the creation of this physical world is to create a dwelling place for Him in this lowly world.

4. See Midrash *Tanchuma*, Parshat, Naso, chapter 16.

5. Rabbi Saadiah Gaon. *Emunot VeDevot*. At the end of the first Maamor. See also Rabbi Shalom Dovber, the fifth Chabad Rebbe. *Safer HaMaamorim. 5666* (New York: Kehot Publication Society, 1971). Yom Tov Shel Rash Hashanah, pp. 7–8.

"*Me'Ayin, Le'Yesh*,"⁶ we have the task to undo and make a "something" into a "nothing."

To briefly explain this concept, we return to that which was previously mentioned. Before God created any of the worlds, including the spiritual worlds above, there was only the *Ein Sof*, the infinite light of God, and through a process of *Tzimtzumim*, constrictions and concealments of the *Ein Sof*, there began the process of *Seder Hishtalshelut*, continuous link, from one level of spirituality to the next, from one world of holiness to the next, finally arriving at the highest level of the world of *Asiyah*, which is the lowest of the spiritual worlds.

In order to create a physical world, limited by dimensions of time and space, something besides this continous link was necessary. This link is part of a continuous chain of spirituality, from one higher level of spirituality to the next, and physicality cannot emerge from spirituality. No matter how many concealments and constrictions of the spiritual, there will not come forth any physical existence. Therefore, it was the essence of God, known as the infinite light, the *Ein Sof* (that part of the divine which exists above the "continuous link"), who created this physical universe. For only He, who is above the link, can create an existence that does not originate from the link, a *physical* existence. Accordingly, we call the creation of the physical *Ex Nihilo*, something from nothing, because the

---

6. *Midrash HaGadol. Genesis* in the beginning. *Ramban. Genesis*, chapter 1, verse 1. *Rambam. The Guide To The Perplexed* (Jerusalem: Mossad Harav Kook, 1977), part 3, chapter 10. Rabbi Schneur Zalman of Liadi. *Tanya. Shar Hayichud VaHaEmuna* (New York: Kehot Publication Society, 1965), chapter 2. Rabbi Dan Yitzchak Abarbanel. *Genesis* in the beginning. "Explanation of the world created." By the same author, *Mifalot Elokim* (Jerusalem: Otzer Hapaskim, 1993), Maamor 2, chapter 5. Rabbi Chayim of Volozhin. *Nefesh HaChayim* (Bnei Brak: 1989), Shar 1, chapter 13, in the note.

physical world is not in or from the continuous link of worlds. This physical world comes from nothingness, from a nonexistence, a noncreation—the *Ein Sof*. (When we speak of nothingness, what we speak of is a positive nothingness, a true nothingness, the non-dimensional, nonphysical, even non-spiritual being, the *Ein Sof*, which is beyond any definition at all.[7]) God created this world in His image, the image of the *Ein Sof*. Just as the *Ein Sof* has no beginning and no origins, it was, is, and will always be. So it is with this physical world. The physical existence feels itself to be "ex nihilo" and, therefore, declares, "My existence is from myself,"[8] physicality proclaims, "I have no creator." This feeling is true in a positive sense, for the world indeed does come from nothingness, the nothingness being the *Ein Sof*, however, the world proclaims it in a negative sense, in the sense that it has no creator. Man has the ability to reverse this. He takes the *Yesh*, the physical existence, the "something," and transforms it into *Ayin*, nothingness, to spirituality which is the true "nothingness."[9]

The Talmud tells us[10] that, through our reciting and proclaiming on the eve of Shabbat that God created the world, we "become partners with God in the creation." He creates from nothingness a physical existence, and we transform the

---

7. Rabbi Moshe Corodovero, *Pardess Rimonim* (Jerusalem: 1962), Shar 23, chapter 1.

8. See Rabbi Schneur Zalman of Liadi, *Tanya* (New York: Kehot Publication Society, 1965), Igerret HaKodesh, letter 20.

9. Since man has the power of the infinite, the power of the *Ein Sof*, he can thus take apart so to speak what the *Ein Sof* created. Rabbi M. M. Schneerson. *Likutei Sichot* (New York: Kehot Publication Society, 1977), Vol. 12. Parshat, Tazria (2), p. 74.

10. Talmud. *Shabbat* 119b. See *Shulchan Aruch HaRav*, Orach Chayim, chapter 268:1.

physical existence into nothingness, into spirituality. Moreover, the Talmud states, "The work and achievements of the righteous are even greater than the accomplishments of the creator."[11]

Thus, the intention of the Godly soul's descent to this world is to elevate the body it inhabits, to elevate and transform the physicality of the world into holiness. The ultimate purpose of the soul's descent is the elevation of the physical body it inhabits; this is the soul's mission and reason for being. Yet God rewards the soul for accomplishing its mission, for God assigns to every creation its appropriate reward. As it states in the Talmud,[12] "God does not withhold rewards from any living creature." The reward of the soul is its elevation. Moreover, the elevation it receives as its reward is an even greater elevation and raises it to even loftier spiritual heights than those experienced by the soul when above. What does it mean when we speak of a soul's elevation, and how is it achieved?

The Kabbalah explains[13] that the purpose of the Godly soul's descent to this world is *Tikkun*, rectification. When we speak of "*Tikkun*," we are speaking of completion. It does not mean to say that the soul has faults and is in need of rectification and purification, rather, *Tikkun* in this instance means that the soul receives an even greater fulfillment[14] becoming more complete than when it was in the spritiual

---

11. See Talmud. *Ketubot* 5a. See Rabbi Yoseph Yitzchak, the sixth Chabad Rebbe. *Safer HaMaamorim 5685* (New York: Kehot Publication Society, 1986), p. 141.

12. The Talmud, numerous times. For instance, *Bava Kamma* 38b, *Nazir* 23b.

13. *Safer Shar HaGilgulim*, Hakdamah 16; *Safer HaGilgulim*, chapter 4: *Shulchan Aruch HaRav*. Hilchot Talmud Torah, chapter 1, Halachah 4.

14. *Safer Shar HaGilgulim*. Hakdamah 1.

worlds above. It is written[15] that the elevation the soul achieves is a new form of attachment, revealed between the soul and God. When the Godly soul dwelled in the spiritual realms, it was in its natural habitat. The connection with Godliness that the soul experienced in that state was natural and instinctive, for there exists only holiness in the spiritual worlds above, and there is no challenge to this connection. The level of attachment the soul has in the spiritual realms is almost a habit. However, when the soul descends to a world which proclaims, "I have no creator, my existence is from myself," and *there* the soul serves and remains connected to God, the soul then reveals a new and deeper relationship with God. For the soul now demonstrates that, even in an unfriendly environment, it still remains closely attached to Godliness. And this attachment is demonstrated through the service of God in this physical world, by serving God through elevating one's entire physicality and one's physical environment to spirituality.

There is a parable that illustrates the above idea. A child was born and raised in a religious commune, situated on a remote island. The practice of the commune was for everyone to serve the master, the holy man, for he was their teacher and their ruler. The master was to them all that they needed and wanted in life. This child we speak of was also taught, from the day he was born, to love and revere the master. When the child grew older, the master had an idea. He de-

---

15. See Rabbi Mayor Eben Aldavie, Shivilei Emunah, Nosiv Tishihei, p. 379 (Jerusalem edition 1990). See Rabbi Yoseph Yitzchak, the sixth Chabad Rebbe, *Safer HaMaamorim* 5706 (New York: Kehot Publication Society, 1986), p. 101. See Rabbi M. M. Schneerson. *Likutei Sichot* (New York: Kehot Publication Society, 1980), Vol. 15, p. 247. See also Rabbi Menasha Ben Israel, *Nishmat Chayim*, Maamor 2, chapter 6.

cided to send this young lad far away on a journey through different cultures and civilizations, so that he should gain greater experiences from the world at large and become a more complete human being. In addition, this journey would serve as a test for this young lad, to see if he truly and wholeheartedly loved and revered the master. On the island, the entire environment was one that nurtured love and reverence for the master; it was natural for the child to do the same. However, in distant lands, the environment is not conducive to these feelings. If the child will continue to love and revere the master as he did on the remote island, it will be proof of his absolute devotion to the master. The same is true with the soul's descent to earth. The advantages of this descent are two-fold: Firstly, the added dimensions of the physical world causes the soul to become more complete and comprehensive; and secondly, the soul can prove its strong connection to Godliness through its service of Him even in a physical world.

Through this descent, the soul becomes, in a sense, infinite. When the soul descends to this earthly sphere, its task is to transform it into a spiritual world. In Hebrew, the world is called (עולם) *Olam*, which contains the same three basic letters of the Hebrew word for concealment, which is *Hel'lem* (העלם).[16] The letters are *Ayin* (ע), *Lamed* (ל), and *Mem* (ם). This world connotes concealment of Godliness. The task of the soul is to change the nature of the world and transform it into a

---

16. See Rabbi Schneur Zalman of Liadi, *Likutei Torah* (New York: Kehot Publication Society, 1996), Prashat, Shelach, p. 37D. See also *Midrash Kohelet*. Parsha 3, chapter 11:3. Talmud. *Pesachim* p. 50a. *Safer HaBahir*, number 10. Rabbi Dan Yitzchak Abarbanel. *Mifalot Elokim* (Jerusalem: Otzer Hapaskim, 1993), Maamor 8, chapter 7. Rabbi Avraham HaMalach (1739–1776). *Chesed LeAvraham* (Jerusalem: Sifsei Tzadikim, 1995), Parshat Emor.

world of revealed Godliness. The soul, therefore, actually breaks the nature of the world; it goes above the world's limitations, beyond its very own nature. In a sense, the world becomes supernatural, *above its nature*. Therefore, the soul receives the same elevation as it gives the world. It attains a limitless and infinite connection with God, a connection that goes beyond the natural.[17]

The Mishnah states, "By force you are living, and by force you shall die."[18] This means that one does not want to come into this life and neither does one desire to leave it. Therefore, it is by force that one lives and passes on. If one does not want to come into life, then there would seem to be no need to force him to leave this world and vice versa. Chassidus explains[19] that this Mishnah is referring to the Godly soul in man. Prior to the soul's descent to this inferior world, the soul cries out, "I don't want to go, why must I leave the presence of Godliness? Why enter a world that is devoid of Godliness? I wish to stay here above in these spiritual worlds and be continuously in the presence of holiness!" This is the soul's protest before its descent to this lowly world. It is in reference to this that the Mishnah states, "By force you are living." Your soul was forced to descend to this world.

However, once the soul does descend and realizes how much it can achieve spiritually and the level of the elevations possible on this lowly universe, it cries when its time in this

---

17. See Rabbi Schneur Zalman of Liadi, *Likutei Torah* (New York: Kehot Publication Society, 1996), Prashat Re'eh, p. 29A.

18. See *Avot*, chapter 4, Mishnah 22.

19. Rabbi Shalom Dovber, the fifth Chabad Rebbe, *Safer HaMaamorim 5659*. (New York: Kehot Publication Society, 1977), pp. 7–8. See also Rabbi Schneur Zalman of Liadi, *Tanya* (New York: Kehot Publication Society, 1965), chapter 50.

world is over and the soul has to depart from its body. Therefore, the Mishnah says, "By force, you are going to die."

(It should be noted that the elevation the soul receives in this world is only applicable to the lower levels of the soul, the *Nefesh*, *Ruach*, and *Neshamah*; however, the level of *Chayah*, and especially the level of *Yichidah*, do not need, and nor can they have, any form of *Tikkun*.[20])

The manner in which the soul achieves this elevation is through the observance of the 613 commandments, the *mitzvot*. It is explained that every individual soul has 613 compartments, and, likewise, there are 613 vessels to receive the 613 parts of the soul. These are the 613 organs and general veins in the human body which absorb the soul.[21] God gave us 613 commandments, corresponding to the 613 compartments. Through the observance of each mitzvah, we elevate the corresponding compartment in the soul. However, in order for each particular mitzvah to elevate the corresponding part in the soul, the mitzvah has to be done as the Talmud states, "carefully and with great intensity and fervor."[22] Furthermore, the mitzvah must be done with all three of the soul's garments: with one's thought, speech, and action.[23] The mitzvah should not only be a simple action, rather it must permeate your entire being, your mind as well as your ability to communicate. Through this, the corresponding part of the soul will be elevated.

The method of *Tikkun* (elevation) is firstly, the elevation of the entire lower level of the soul, the *Nefesh*. This level of

---

20. *Safer Shar HaGilgulim*, Hakdamah 1.
21. Reb Hayim Vital, *Sharei Kedushah*, chapter 1, Shar 1.
22. Talmud. *Shabbat* 118b.
23. See *Safer Shar HaGilgulim*, Hakdamah 11. See Rabbi Schneur Zalman of Liadi, *Tanya* (New York: Kehot Publication Society, 1965), Igerret HaKodesh, Letter, 29.

soul which is analogous to the world of *Asiyah*, which, as explained in the Kabbalah,[24] contains all five levels of the soul (each one of the five levels of soul has in itself five subdivisions). Accordingly, the level of *Nefesh* has the *Nefesh* of *Nefesh*, the *Ruach* of *Nefesh*, and *Neshamah* of *Nefesh* (and even the *Chayah* and *Yichidah* of *Nefesh*). After a person has elevated his or her entire level of *Nefesh*, with all its five subdivisions—through doing all 613 *mitzvot*, with great caution and vigilance—only then, with much effort and, as Rabbi Hayim Vital writes,[25] "Through great difficulties and travail" (and only if he is meritorious enough) will God exchange his soul of *Nefesh* (which at this point is completely elevated) for a higher level of soul, the level of *Ruach*, corresponding to the higher world of *Yetzirah*. And if he elevates the entire level of *Ruach*—with all its subdivisions—he can then elevate the higher level of soul, the level of *Neshamah*. (The level of *Chayah* and *Yichidah* cannot have and do not need any form of elevation.)

The above-mentioned process, however, only refers to the majority of people. These people have "ordinary souls." However, there are those who have a higher level of soul, the "truly new soul" (which is above the "general soul of Adam,"[26] as will be explained in the following paragraph). It is easy, almost effortless for the people who contain this soul to reach the levels above *Nefesh*, to reach *Ruach*, *Neshamah*, and even *Chayah* and *Yichidah*. Furthermore, it is most likely that, when these souls descend to this earth to inhabit a human form, they will not sin and will be truly righ-

---

24. See *Safer Shar HaGilgulim*, Hakdamah 1. See *Safer Sader HaGilgulim*, Ma-Asei Noraim.
25. *Safer Shar HaGilgulim*, Hakdamah 3.
26. *Ibid*. Hakdamah 7 and Hakdamah 32.

teous people.[27] However, this is not a guarantee that they will never sin; it is only more likely because they are inclined by their nature to do good.

In the Kabbalah, it is explained[28] that when God created the primordial man, Adam, the first of all human beings, the entire course of future mankind was contained within him. All the generations that would come from him were contained within him. Adam was neither male nor female. Adam's body was a synthesis of a male and a female, as the Torah states, "And God created man (Adam) . . . male and female He created them."[29] In his genes, there were embodied the genes of all of mankind until the end of time. He was the all-encompassing being. Adam was the physical father and mother of all mankind.[30]

And just as he was the physical father and mother of mankind, the Kabbalah explains that Adam was also the spiritual parent of mankind. Adam's soul is the general soul "from whence all souls emanate."[31]

The physical structure of Adam, the form of his body, was in a sense analogous to the spiritual form of Adam. The physical dimensions of Adam's body were parallel to the

---

27. *Ibid.* Hakdamah 6. See Talmud. *Bava Metzia* 61A, "You—God—have created the righteous" (see *Tanya,* chapter 14).
28. *Safer Shar HaGilgulim,* Hakdamah 6.
29. See *Genesis,* chapter 1, verse 27. See Talmud. *Eruvin* 18a.
30. See Rabbi Yehudah Loew, *Tifferet Yisrael* (Israel: 1980), at the end of chapter 47.
31. Even the first level of souls (which we said are above Adam) have a connection with "this general soul of Adam." See Hakdamah 12 in the beginning. All souls originate from the general soul of Adam. See also *Midrash Rabbah. Exodus.* Parsha 40, chapter 3. *Midrash Tanchuman.* Parshat Ki Tissa 12. Rabbi Schneur Zalman of Liadi, *Tanya. Igeret HaKodesh* (New York: Kehot Publication Society, 1965), letter 7.

structure of his soul, which is the "general soul." Therefore, the Kabbalah teaches that there are souls whose source is from the *head* of Adam, and there are souls whose source is from the *hands* of Adam, and so on. (In practical terms, this means that those souls whose roots are from the *head* of Adam are the *intellectual* parts of the general soul and, therefore, inclined toward intellect. And those souls whose roots are from the *hands* of the general soul are more inclined to physical activity, and so on. The Talmud says, "When Adam was created, he reached from the heavens above to the earth below, however, after Adam sinned, God decreased his body,"[32] which is to say that his physical dimensions—his body—as well as his spiritual dimensions—his soul—were diminished. In a spiritual sense, this means the parts of his soul that were parallel to the parts of his body that were diminished were also diminished, and these souls "fell off his body and fell into the unholy." These souls are called "the old souls." The parts of his soul that stayed "attached" to his body (we speak here in anthropomorphic terms) are called, in the Kabbalah, "the new souls," and the souls that are above Adam are called "truly new souls."

These are the three types of souls.

The souls of most human beings today are the new souls.[33] These 'new souls,' from the soul of Adam, were later split into two divisions, corresponding to Adam's two sons. One division is the soul connected to Abel, which contains souls that stem from *Chesed*—kindness, grace, and benevolence, and the second division contains the souls that are connected to Cain, corresponding to *Gevurah*—might, power, prevalence.)

---

32. See Talmud. *Sanhedrin* 38b, *Chagigah* 12a. *D'Rebbe Eliezer* chapter 11.
33. *Safer Shar HaGilgulim*, Hakdamah 3.

In order for these new souls to reach the next level of soul, that of *Ruach*, they must first elevate their entire dimension of *Nefesh*. Moreover, these higher reaches of soul can be attained only through great difficulties. However, those with the level of 'old souls' can attain the higher level of soul, *Ruach*, even without elevating the entire *Nefesh*. (However, in order for this to transpire, they must first recite the "prayer of repentance," with focused intention.[34])

This is the advantage of the 'old souls' over the 'new souls,' for the former can elevate the level of *Ruach* before their *Nefesh* has been refined. However, even these souls cannot reach the next level of *Neshamah*, until they first elevate their entire level of *Ruach*.[35] (There is yet another level of soul, and that is the soul of convert.)[36] However, once converted, he receives a Godly soul, a soul whose source is holiness.[37]

We spoke of the soul's descent to the physical world and its journey of *Tikkun*. The quest for *Tikkun* is an ardous and formidable one. Many live an entire lifetime without experiencing a total elevation of soul. If one had lived an entire

---

34. See *Ibid*, Hakdamah 7.
35. See *Ibid*.
36. See *Ibid*. Hakdamah 12, 13. See, however, Rabbi Yitzchak of Acco, *Meirat Einayim*. Parshat Bereishit 4:1. Rabbi Nathan Shapiro (1585–1633), *Megalah Amukhot*, on Torah, Parshat Vayeshev, chapter 101. (See also *Megalah Amukhot*, chapter 88.) Rabbi Mayor Eben Aldavie, *Shivilei Emunah*, Nosiv Shelishei (Jerusalem edition 1990), p. 129. And see also *Siddur Rabbi Yakov Emdin*. The laws on the night of *Shabbos*. Where they write, that souls of Jewish converts are Jewish to begin with. Thus, throughout the Talmud, when it mentions a conversion it says, "A *convert* who converted." (See Talmud. *Yivomot* 22a) indicating that he is considered a convert even before he actually converts. See also: Rabbi Yehudah Loew, *Tifferet Yisrael* (Israel: 1980), at the end of chapter 2.
37. See *Ibid*. Hakdamah 34.

life and not elevated the soul to all levels possible, then in order to reach its total elevations, the soul must reincarnate into another human form, until the soul becomes completely elevated. It is significant to note that when the soul descends into this world to be elevated, it is a *reward* for its descent and is *not the purpose of its descent*. The purpose of the descent is to elevate the body, the physical. The elevations of the soul are only a reward for descending to elevate the physical.

3
The Afterlife of the Soul

A soul journeyed to the world below to give life and spirit to a human form. For a lifetime the soul struggled to draw Godliness into a world where it seemed devoid. When its time came to depart its earthly form, the soul returned to its home in the heavenly spheres. However, the soul had not yet elevated itself to its full capacity and it is decreed that the soul must reincarnate into a new body to complete what was left unfinished. This is quite perplexing, as it seems to contradict a basic tenet of Jewish thought, that of reward and punishment after death. If the soul must be reincarnated, when does it receive its reward? It is commonly known that the righteous receive their reward in *Gan Eden*, and the sinners, their punishment in *Gehenom*. However, if immediately following one's death, his soul is reincarnated, how will it receive what it is due? One may think that this contradiction can be reconciled by saying that the soul first receives its reward in *Gan Eden*, and after receiving it, it then descends for its reincarnation. However, this explanation does not resolve the problem, for *Gan Eden* is not a limited reward that expires after a time. In Paradise itself, the souls continuously have elevations. From one level of holiness, they ascend to higher levels of holiness. As the Talmud says, "The righteous souls have no relaxation even in the 'World to Come.'"[1]

It is explained[2] that the immediate relatives of the deceased recite the Kaddish as to assist the deceased soul with its appropriate elevations within *Gan Eden* itself. Every time the Kaddish is recited, the soul above ascends to a higher spiritual level. And the same holds true with the non-righteous people. Immediately after their deaths, they may go to *Gehenom*; nevertheless, through the recital of the Kaddish here below, they are also being continuously elevated from the lower levels of *Gehenom*, until they too reach Paradise.[3]

---

1. Talmud. *Berachot* 64a.

2. According to the Ari Zal, Kaddish assists in the elevation of the soul, within Gan Eden—Paradise, itself. See *Siddur Ari-Zal* before the prayer, "Aleinu." *Kisvie Ari-Zal*, Shar HaKavanot, Kaddish. *Aruch HaSulchan*, Yoreh Deah, chapter 376:12. See also *Shulchan Aruch*. Yoreh Deah, at the end of chapter 376, the commentaries *Lerhem HaPanim* and *Sheyurei Berachah*.

3. See Rabbi Yoseph Caro, *Shulchan Aruch*. Yoreh Deah, chapter 376:4, in the glossary by Rabbi Moshe Isserles; The *Ramah*. The commentaries on the *Tur Shulchan Aruch*. Yoreh Deah, chapter 376, relate a story. (See *Beit Yoseph. Darchei Moshe*. Ad loc. In the name of the Talmud Tractate. *Kallah. Midrash Tanchuma*.) Once Rabbi Akiva met a distressed wondering soul, who told him, that if the living recite Kaddish for the benefit of his soul, they would elevate his soul from *Gehenom*. (The source of this legend is not to be found today in our prints of Talmud not Midrash. See, however, *Kallah Rabti*, chapter 2. *Zohar*, part 1, p. 62b.) Thus, Kaddish is recited to help elevate the soul of the deceased. See *Rabbeinu Bachya. Deuteronomy*, chapter 21, verse 8. *Kall Bo*, chapter 114. *Responsa, Rivash*, chapter 115. *Menorat HaMaor* (Jerusalem: 1961), p. 51. Rabbi Menasha Ben Israel, *Nishmat Chayim*. Maamor 2, chapter 27.

Therefore, how is it possible that the soul is continuously being elevated in *Gan Eden* while, simultaneously, reincarnated and inhabiting another person's body? The question remains, where is the soul after death? (When speaking in spatial terms regarding something spiritual such as the soul, it does not refer to an actual place or time, rather, a state of being.)

Furthermore, at the time of the resurrection of the dead, how will the original body be resurrected without a soul? *Will it* be resurrected? Perhaps only one of the bodies will be resurrected?

A solution to these dilemmas presents itself once we fully understand the process of the soul's elevations.[4]

As explained, the manner in which the soul reaches its proper elevations, is through doing all the 613 commandments with extreme focus and intensity.

As the Talmud[5] says, Rav Joseph once asked the son of the distinguished talmudic sage Rova, "Which of the *mitzvot* was your father's 'special Mitzvah,' which mitzvah did he do with extraordinary care?" He answered, "The mitzvah of *Tzitzit*." This was a special mitzvah for Rova, the most important of all other *mitzvot*. The Talmud[6] declares, "*Every Jew* is full of *mitzvot*." We know that this is not possible in the literal sense, thus, we interpret this statement to mean that every Jew has one particular mitzvah that he feels most connected to, that he feels is *his* mitzvah, and he is "full" of that mitzvah. For example, the mitzvah of giving charity,

---

4. See *Safer Shar HaGilgulim*, Hakdamah 4 and 14. See Rabbi M. M. Schneerson. *Igrot Kodesh* (New York: Kehot Publication Society, 1988), Vol. 2, Letter 200, p. 73.
5. See Talmud. *Shabbat* 118b.
6. See Talmud. *Chagigah* 27a.

helping the poor, or praying. We say that, through this one particular mitzvah, he elevates the one part of his soul—one of the 613 parts—that corresponds to that particular mitzvah.[7]

Now, we can begin to understand how the soul can be in "two places at once." For the part of the soul that one personally elevates, that which he was especially connected to in his lifetime, never reincarnates. It is your soul, a distinct and unique soul. It is the real you. The other parts of the soul, those which were not elevated in the individual's lifetime, and he did not come in contact with, has no real connection with the individual. Although it existed within him, throughout his entire lifetime, on a conscious level, he was only connected to the part of the soul that he acted with, which was elevated. For example, an individual who is considered a kind and loving person, a person of *Chesed* and charity, is connected to, and therefore elevates, the part of the soul which corresponds to the mitzvah of charity. Furthermore, the way he served God was through love and thus he connected and elevated yet another part of his soul, which corresponds to the mitzvah of loving God. When people think of this individual, they remember him always as a "loving human being." For this is what he truly was, a person connected with the level of *Chesed* within his soul (which is one of the 613 parts of the entire soul), corresponding to the mitzvah of *Chesed*—charity; loving God and in extension loving man.[8] Therefore, we say that, on a conscious level, he is a person of *Chesed*, although within his soul there is contained all levels of *Gevurah*.

---

7. Rabbi Avraham Azulay, *Chesed LeAvraham*, part 5, chapter 21.
8. The Lubavitcher Rebbe, *Sefer Ha'Maamorim Meluket* (New York: Kehot Publication Society, 1987), vol. 1, p. 36.

This loving individual of whom we spoke above may also be a person who does all the rest of the 612 *mitzvot*; however, all the other *mitzvot* that he does are done as an extension of the mitzvah of loving (God and man). Even the mitzvah of "fearing God" (which stems from Gevurah, the opposite of love in the *Sefirot*) is done as an extension of his love for God. He fears God, not because he feels himself small and distant from God; on the contrary, he fears God because of his love for Him. He loves God so much, he will do whatever God asks of him, and if God wills him to fear Him, he will fear, because he loves God and wants to do exactly what He desires.[9] Moreover, his fear of God is a fear of rejection, being unloved.

And the opposite is also true. If one is a person who serves God through Gevurah, through fear, he can also love God out of fear. Because he fears Him, he will feel whatever God demands, he will even love.

It is this part of the individual's soul, the part that was his distinct part, the "me" of the soul, that goes to *Gan Eden* (or otherwise), and it is with this portion of soul that he will be resurrected. The parts of the soul that do reincarnate into another human being are the parts of the soul that were never elevated, that had no connection with any of its previous bodies on a conscious level. These parts of the soul reincarnate until they are completely elevated, thus it can take up to 613 different individuals to elevate all 613 parts of the lowest level the *Nefesh* (and sometimes even more than that). Although these parts of the soul were also present within the individual's body, since however he never experienced any

---

9. Rabbi Joseph Albo, *Safer Haikkarim*, Maamor 3, chapter 34. There is fear which is an extension of love.

contact with them, and they were never elevated and activated. Thus, they are not considered to be his at all, even though they were somewhere deep down in his subconscious. They were present, but not as a part of his personality.

From the above, we surmise that the first person to receive a soul (i.e., an unused and never reincarnated soul) receives a complete soul with all 613 compartments intact. However, after his demise, the parts of the soul that became exclusively his remain in the upper worlds, and only the remainder of the soul reincarnates. Does this mean that the future bodies that this soul will inhabit will receive an incomplete soul?

In a sense, this question refers to all owners of this particular soul, including the original individual. At the time of the resurrection of the dead, each of the inhabitants will only have a part of this soul. Will they be incomplete? The explanation is[10] as follows. Just as the general soul of Adam has 613 general compartments, so, too, all the individual souls that stem from this general soul have within them 613 compartments. Each of those compartments have within them 613 compartments, and this continues into infinity. From this, we learn that the soul is truly an infinite creation.

It is known in Kabbalah that the Godly soul of man "is truly a part of God,"[11] which translates as being part of some-

---

10. See Rabbi M. M. Schneerson. *Igrot Kodesh* (New York: Kehot Publication Society, 1988), volume 2. Letter 200, for a detailed explanation.

11. This concept of soul is based on the words of the Ramban, who writes that since the creation of man it says "And He blew into his nostrils a breath of life." (*Genesis*, chapter 2, verse 7.) Thus, whoever blows, blows from his inner essence. Hence, man's soul is from the inner being of God. See *Ramban*, on *Genesis*, chapter 2, verse 7. *Kisvei HaRamban, Derashot. Toraht Hashem Temimah* (Jerusalem: Mossad Harav Kook, 1982), p. 159. Rabbi Shabtai Sheftel Horowitz (1565–1619) writes, "the soul of man is part of God." *Shefa Tal* in the introduc-

thing infinite. No matter how many times one divides infinite, it will always remain infinite. It will still remain complete, for the infinite is indivisible. When you grasp just a bit of the infinite, you grasp the whole."[12]

I once heard it said that, in the Sinai desert, there is a large rock shaped in a very peculiar fashion. The interesting thing

---

tion. See also, Rabbi Moshe Corodovero, *Pardess Rimonim*. Shar 32, chapter 1, in the beginning Or Ne'erov (Israel: 1965), part 1, chapter 3, p. 8. Rabbi Avraham Azulay, *Chesed LeAvraham*. part 2, chapter 44. Rabbi Yoseph Yavatz (London: HaMatfis, 1953) on *Avot*, chapter 1, Mishnah 17; and chapter 3, Mishnah 19. Rabbi Schneur Zalman of Liadi, *Tanya* (New York: Kehot Publication Society, 1965), chapter 2. Rabbi Menacham Mendel of Vitebsk. (?–1788) *Pri HaAretz*. (Jerusalem: HaMsorah, 1989), Parshat Vayeshev. Rabbi Moshe Chayim Luzzatto. *Da'at Tevunoth*, in the beginning. Rabbi Yonathan Eibeschuvetz Yarot D'Vash (Jerusalem: Levin-Epstain) part 1, p. 8b. Rabbi Menochem Zaoryah De Fano Moomor Hanefesh part 3, chapter 8. See also Rabbi Chayim of Volozhin, *Nefesh HaChayim* (Bnei Brak: 1989), Shar 1, chapter 15.

Philosophers have argued, that to say "a part of God" is an oxymoron, for how can there be a part of something indivisible? (See Rabbi Menasha Ben Israel, *Nishmat Chayim*. Maamor 2, chapter 9. Rabbi Schneur Zalman of Liadi, *Tanya*. *Igeret HaKodesh*. Letter 7, in another context.) Nonetheless, when there is an argument, in whatever subject, one must decide according to the experts in that particular field. Thus, with regards to the soul, the verdict lies with the mystics. See, The Lubavitcher Rebbe, *Igrot Kodesh* (New York: Kehot Publication Society, 1989), vol. 10, p. 353. A great Chassidic master once said, "That for God to create ex nihilo, something—Yesh creation, existence, from nothing —Godliness, is not a monumental act. For God can surely do anything. However, man does observe God's greatness in the creation of souls. Where He creates a soul, an existence, a Yesh, while still remaining an Ayin—nothingness, i.e.: part of God; the entity of soul, is a complete contradiction; a Yesh—existence—and Ayin—nonexistence—all part of one reality."

12. Rabbi Shalom Dovber, the fifth Chabad Rebbe, *Safer HaMaamorim 5669* (New York: Kehot Publication Society, 1981), p. 73. By the same rebbe, *Yom Tov Shel Rosh Hashanah 5666* (New York: Kehot Publication Society, 1972), p. 522. Keter Shem Tov (New York: Kehot Publication Society, 1972), chapter 111, and Hosofot 116. See also Rabbi Yaakov Yoseph of Polonnye (?–1784). *Toldot Yaakov Yoseph*. Parshat Yitro. Rabbi Yoseph Yavatz (London: HaMatfis, 1953), on *Avot*, chapter 4, Mishnah 2.

about this rock is that all the smaller stones of the rock are shaped exactly like the general rock. Thus, if you look at the rock as a whole, you see one shape, and then when you take a small piece from the rock, you will see that it looks exactly like the entire rock.[13]

In fractal geometry, there is an equation ($Z2 + C$) that has amazing results. This equation is known as "the Mandelbrot Set." When this equation is converted to computer graphics, it produces a strange geometrical shape. It looks like a large circle in the shape of a heart, connected with a smaller circle, with web-like shapes all around it. What is fascinating about this is that, when you go to any point in the entire set and magnify the point, you will see an exact replica of the original set reproduced. And this equation can be done infinitely. No difference how many times you zoom into the set, you will always see this same equation. This is called mathematical infinity.

The same holds true with all parts of the soul. No matter how many times the soul divides itself, it will always contain the shape and form of a general soul—it always has all 613 compartments. As a result, each soul in its own right is a complete soul.

On a practical level, this means that each person's soul is completely comprehensive, and the fact that one's personality and thus his main connection to his soul, is one of kindness—*Chesed*—does not mean that he is missing the level of *Gevurah* (fear and awe of God). It does mean, however, that this person's fear of God stems from his love.

---

13. See Rabbi Tzadok Hacohen of Lublin (1823–1890), *Sichot Malacei Hasharot*. (Bnei Brak: Yehadut, 1973), chapter 3, p. 42, Rabbi Yokov Emdin, *Migdal Oz*. Aliyot Ha'tevah, p. 240.

Throughout the ages, man has served God in many different ways. There have been periods in history when God was viewed as a fearsome Master and the relationship between man and his God was based on fear. There have been other eras that were eras of awe, when God inspired awe in His creations and their service of Him was based on their humility before Him. Starting with the *Baal Shem Tov*, the holy master of Chassidus, love became the focus of our relationship with God. The methods of serving God have also varied over time. In the times of the Temple, for example, sacrifices were the way of service, and today it is prayer.[14]

From a purely physical standpoint, this can be explained as simple evolution of man. Historians may view the past as natural occurrences—shaped by nature. However, everything on this physical plane has a parallel explanation in the higher worlds. History must be seen as multidimensional, rather than surface level. Viewing the variations in the functions of Godly service on a deeper plane, in a spiritual outlook, we begin to understand this as something different and actually related to the souls of man.

Throughout history, God has wanted different relationships with His creations and different elevations at various periods of time. In order to achieve this, the souls He sent down at that time were generally of a certain nature. For example, when God desired a loving relationship with His creations, the souls that were sent to inhabit bodies in that

---

14. See Talmud. *Berachot*, p. 26a. And see Rambam, *The Guide to the Perplexed* (Jerusalem: Mossad Harav Kook, 1977), part 3, chapter 32. Where the Rambam explains that the inner reason why today there exist prayers in the place of sacrifices, is not only coincidental, rather, primarily it has to do with a different stage in the development of mankind.

era were all souls whose main connection (personality, if you will) was one of *Chesed*—kindness and love and so on.[15]

We have just established that every single individual being, even the wicked, has its special *mitzvot* that he is connected to. Through the mitzvah, an individual elevates one part of his soul. This is the part of soul that he lived with; therefore, it is this soul that is his soul forever. It is the *you* that, after death, will either receive its rewards or the opposite. The Mishnah states,[16] "Every single Jew has a portion in the world to come." The commentaries explain,[17] the world to come refers to the time of resurrection, and every single Jew will be resurrected.

Chassidus explains[18] that the resurrection of the physical body will be the reward for the actual doing of the *mitzvot*. We do the action of the mitzvah with our physical bodies; hence, the reward the body receives is the resurrection of the body. Every single person has his special mitzvah to which he is most connected and which he does with special care and intensity, thus it is understood why the Mishnah proclaims, "every single Jew has a portion in the world to come." Everyone has his special mitzvah, his distinct soul. With that soul, he will be resurrected.

Most people manage to elevate at least one part of their soul throughout their entire lives. The other parts of the soul that were not elevated reincarnate to other human beings. However, if a person succeeds to elevate the entire level of

---

15. See Rabbi Schneur Zalman of Liadi. *Tanya* (New York: Kehot Publication Society, 1965), *Igeret HaKodesh*, Letter 7.
16. See *Sanhedrin*, chapter 10, Mishnah 1.
17. See *Ibid*. The commentary *Bartinoro* by Rabbi Ovadia (1445–1515).
18. Rabbi Shalom Dovber, the fifth Chabad Rebbe, *Safer HaMaamorim 5672* (New York: Kehot Publication Society, 1977), vol. 3, p. 1212.

Nefesh, through great difficulty and travail, it is possible for God to bestow upon him the higher level of *Ruach* which he will then in turn attempt to elevate.

There is a monumental difference between souls from the highest level—"The *truly* new souls"—and the majority of souls—"The new souls." If one's soul is from the "truly new souls," then it is conceivable for there to be contained within him all three of levels of the soul, the *Nefesh*, *Ruach*, and *Neshamah*, at the same time.[19] However if one's soul is from the "new souls"; then, once the entire level of *Nefesh* has been elevated, and one has received the level of *Ruach* the level of *Nefesh*—which by now is totally elevated—departs the body. Therefore, one has only the level of *Ruach*, and the same will hold true if one elevates the entire *Ruach*. Nevertheless, once all the levels of soul have been elevated, it is possible for all three levels (the elevated *Nefesh*, *Ruach*, and *Neshamah*) to come together and permeate one's body simultaneously.[20] (Even the "truly new souls" cannot attain the level of *Ruach* until they reach the age of 13. Neither can they attain the level of *Neshamah* until they reach the age of 20.)[21]

The manner in which a new soul receives a higher level of soul can be either one of two ways: one is through great difficulty and travail and the other is through *Yibum*. Yibum is a law in the Torah which dictates that when a man dies and leaves no offspring, his brother must marry the widow and produce children with her in order to continue the brother's name. The Torah considers this a new edifice.

---

19. *Safer Shar HaGilgulim*, Hakdamah 2.
20. See *Ibid.*, Hakdamah 2, 3.
21. See *Ibid.*, Hakdamah 2. Rabbi Avraham Azulay. *Chesed LeAvraham* part 5, chapter 20.

According to the Kabbalah, it means he will be considered a new man. It is as if he attains now at the time of marriage a new soul. Therefore, the Kabbalah explains, just as the "truly new souls" can elevate all three parts of the soul in one body (they all can be present throughout the entire elevation; the lower levels of soul do not depart the body when the higher levels enter) and they can elevate these higher levels without difficulties, so too these "new human beings." They can elevate the level of *Ruach*, without any difficulties,[22] and they can elevate the highest levels of *Neshamah*, while at the same time, the lowest levels of *Nefesh* are still contained within them.[23]

For the majority of people, the transition between the *Nefesh* leaving the body and the *Ruach* entering it is a very difficult one and requires much hard work and travail. Therefore, it is conceivable that an individual who has elevated his level of *Nefesh*, and now stands on the threshold of receiving *Ruach*, may decide that he is satisfied with his level of spirituality (soul) as it stands and does not want to go through the hardships necessary to receive *Ruach*. This person now has a problem: he has no soul. His *Nefesh* has left and he is not receiving the *Ruach*. How does this person exist? The Kabbalah[24] explains that in this scenario, *Ibbur* occurs, which is to say, the level of *Ruach* from a departed *Tzaddik*, even from as far back as the times of the patriarchs, descends down to inhabit the body and becomes his soul. (This will be further explained in Chapter 6.)

---

22. *Ibid.* (However, in *Safer Gilgulim*, Sader Gilgulim questions the idea, if through *Yibum* a new soul can become like a truly new soul and elevate *Ruach* and *Neshamah* even without difficulties.)

23. *Ibid.* Hakdamah 2,3.

24. *Ibid.* Hakdamah 2.

Once all three compartments of the soul, with all its 613 subdivisions, have been totally elevated, the soul will not return to this world. It will never again be reincarnated into another human being.[25]

The souls of the wicked, says the Kabbalah, do not reincarnate more than three times.[26] This is explained by the following scenario: A soul descended to this physical world for the first time, and the person whom it inhabited was completely wicked and a moral and did not elevate even

---

25. A great Chassidic Rebbe would tell his disciples that they should aspire to accomplish all they can in this lifetime, since this may be the last generation before the redemption, and then there will be no more reincarnations. See Rabbi Tzadok Hacohen of Lublin, *Pri Tzadik* (Bnei Brak: Yehadut, 1973), Mishpatim 3. Rabbi Mordecai Yoseph of Izhbitz (1801–1854), *Mei Hashiluch* (Israel: Mishor, 1995), book 2, p. 283.

26. See *Zohar*, part 3, p. 72b. *Zohar*, part 2, p. 91b. *Tikunei Zohar*, Tikkun 32, p. 76b. *Tikunei Zohar*, Tikkun 70, p. 138a. Rabbi Moshe ben Nachman, Ramban *Kisvei HaRamban* (Jerusalem: Mossad Harav Kook, 1982), *Job* p. 101. See footnote 30. Ad loc. Rabbeinu Bachya. *Kad HaKemach* (Jerusalem: Mossad Harav Kook, 995), Hasgacha, p. 151. *Ma'arechet Elokut* (Jerusalem: 1963), chapter 10. Author unknown. There are those who attribute this text to Rabbi Todros Halevi Abulafia (1220–1298). See Rabbi Moshe Corodovero, *Pardess Rimonim*. Shar 6, chapter 2. Others attribute this text to Rabbi Peretz Hacohen, one of the authors of Tosefot. See The Lubavitcher Rebbe, *Likutei Sichot* (New York: Kehot Publication Society, 1980), Vol. 16, p. 491. Rabbi Menachem *Recanti*. *Genesis*. Parshat Vayeshev. Rabbi Yitzchak of Acco. *Meirat Einayim*. Parshat Bereishit 4:1. Rabbi Mayer Eben Aldavia. *Shivilei Emunah*. Nosiv Thishihei (Jerusalem: 1990) p. 401. Rabbi Yoseph Caro, *Maggid Mesharim* (Jerusalem: Orah, 1960), *Job*, p. 164. Rabbi Moshe, *Alshich*. (1508–1600) *Deuteronomy*, chapter 7, verses 9, 10. Rabbi Eliezer Ezcary, *Safer Cheraidim*, chapter 33. Rabbi Chayim Vital. *Safer Shar HaGilgulim*. Hakdamah 4. Rabbi Naphtali Hirtz Bacharach. *Emek HaMelech*. Hakdamah 2, chapter 3. Rabbi Avraham Azulay. *Chesed LeAvraham*, part 5, chapter 19. Rabbi Meir Ben Gabbai. *Avodat Hakodesh*. Part 2. Chapter 32. Rabbi Menasha Ben Israel. *Nishmat Chayim*. Maamor 4, chapter 14. The *MaHarsha*. On Talmud. *Shabbat*, p. 152b. VeHoyto Nefesh. All these opinions are in agreement, that a wicked soul will only reincarnate three times.

one part of the soul.[27] It then came down again for a second and third time. All three times it inhabited the body of a wicked person, and none of these three individuals elevated even one part of the soul. This soul will never come down again to be reincarnated. After three times, the soul becomes cut off.[28] The soul dissolves into nothingness. (However, only the lower parts of the soul, the *Nefesh*, can get cut off. The higher parts of the soul—*Ruach* and *Neshamah*—can never be cut off.[29] Therefore, if they were not elevated in the first, second, or third time, they can still be reincarnated for as many times as is needed to be totally elevated.)

The soul will only be cut off if every one of the three individuals who contained it did not elevate even one part of it; however, if one of these people elevated even one part of the *Nefesh*, then the soul can be reincarnated, up until 1,000 times.[30] The idea of a soul being "cut off," after three times, does not mean that it becomes completely cut off and expires into total nothingness,[31] rather, as explained,[32] that a human

---

27. His personality, therefore, came from a different source other than his godly soul. His animalistic soul was the soul which gave him life.

28. See *Safer Shar HaGilgulim*. Hakdamah 4. See also *Safer HaGilgulim*, chapter 6. *Zohar Chadash*. Parsat Ki Tetze, p. 107.

29. See *Safer HaGilgulim*, chapter 6.

30. See *Safer Shar HaGilgulim*. Hakdamah 4.

31. For since the soul of man is a part of God, thus it is eternal. See Rabbi Moshe ben Nachman. *Ramban, Shar Hagmul*. Rabbeinu Bachya. *Leviticus*. Parsha Acharei, chapter 18, verse 29. Rabbi Naphtali Hirtz Bacharach. *Emek HaMelech*. Tikunei HaTeshuva 3. Rabbi Dan Yitzchak Abarbanel. *Numbers*. Parshat Shelach. *Midrash Shemuel*. Introduction to *Avot*. Rabbi Menasha Ben Israel. *Nishmat Chayim*. Maamor 1, chapter 4. See also Rabbi Bachya Ibn Pakudah. *Torat HaNefesh*, chapters 1, 7.

32. See Rabbi Yeshayah Halevi Horowitz. *Shallah HaKodesh*. Shnei Luchot Habrit. Parsat Ki Tetze. See Rabbi M. M. Schneerson, *Igrot Kodesh* (New York: Kehot Publication Society, 1987), volume 1, Letter 85, p. 141.

soul after attempting three times to be elevated in a human form will not come down again into another human being, rather, into a lower creature, as will be explained in the next chapter. Or, as it stated in the Kabbalah,[33] a soul that was not elevated in three tries will not descent *alone* to inhabit a human form (to be the soul at birth of a human being). It will however come down again to this world, and inhabit an already existing human being, most likely a righteous tzadik.

From the above we conclude that the soul is multi-faceted. In it is contained the part of the soul that belongs exclusively to the individual, the *you of the soul*, which never reincarnates (although there are rare times when it does indeed reincarnate for specific reasons). And in it, it also has contained the parts of the soul that were not yet elevated, which will reincarnate many times, until it is completely elevated.[34]

---

33. *Safer Shar HaGilgulim*. Hakdamah 5.
34. Rabbi Nathan Shapiro. *Megalah Amukhot*, at the end of chapter 251.

4
Reincarnation as Punishment or *Tikkun*

Reincarnation from one body to another is a long and arduous quest for *tikkun* which the soul undergoes tens, even hundreds of times before it finally achieves its ultimate perfection and receives its rewards. In the previous chapters we discussed this journey of the soul for the purpose of *tikkun*. In the following chapters we will explore other grounds for reincarnation and its manifestations.

If a soul sins while inhabiting a physical body, it receives its appropriate punishments in the realm of *Gehenom*.[1]

---

1. See *Joshua* chapter 15, verse 8. *Jeremiah* chapter 7, verse 31. *Isaiah* chapter 30, verse 33. Here it is written that in a valley neighboring the city of Jerusalem called Gehenom, idol worshipers would burn their own children. For this reason the term Gehenom is used as a metaphor for the punishments for the afterlife. Many commentaries assert that Gehenom is actually a place on this physical planet, with a physical dimension. The reason, however, we don't see it, is because we do not perceive spirituality. It is a spiritual world located in a physical sphere, and occupies physical space. Yet, we can stand right in the

When we speak of God punishing, it does not mean "pay-back time," rather it is a time of refinement and cleansing for the soul. It releases the soul from all its impurities collected in this lowly world, so that the soul can be purified and enter Eternal Paradise. The punishments the soul receives in *Gehenom* are a direct manifestation of the lawless actions it has done in this world. The sin is the action, which causes a reaction. Punishment is caused by the law of cause and effect.[2]

In the Talmud and Midrash, it speaks of a *Gehenom* of flaming fire (which is the most popular vision of "hell" in Western culture) and a *Gehenom* of freezing waters.[3] (This does not mean a literal fire or water,[4] rather a spiritual entity, a spiritual existence devoid of physical dimensions. We use

---

center of Gehenom (or *Gan Eden*) and not feel its presence, because we do not see or feel these higher realities. The following are of the opinion that it has a physical place. *Rambam, Sanhedrin* chapter 10, Mishnah 1. Ramban *Toraht Ha-Adam*. Sharr Hagmul. *Ramban, Genesis* chapter 3, verse 22. Rabbi Chasdai Cresces, *Or Hashem*, Maamor 4, Derush 9. Rabbi Avraham ben HaRambam, *Bereishit* chapter 2, verse 8. Rabbi Nisan ben Reuven. *Derashot HaRan* (Jerusalem: Mochon Sholom, 1977), Derush 7. Rabbi Mayer Eben Aldavis, *Shivilei Emunah* (Jerusalem: 1990). Nosiv Tishihei.

Hence, since Gehenom has a connection to the physical reality, in order for a person to receive his fitting refinement in Gehenom, there remains, even after death, a refined version of the physical body. See *Zohar* part 3, p. 185b. Rabbi Meir Ben Gabbai, *Avodat Hakodesh* part 2, chapter 31. Rabbi Chayim Vital, *Sharei Kedushah*, part 1, Shar 1. Rabbi Menasha Ben Israel. *Nishmat Chayim*. Maamor 1, chapter 10.

2. See Rabbi Yeshayah Halevi Horowitz, *Shallah HaKodesh*. Shnei Luchot Habrit Beit Acharon 12 (1–2). See Rabbi M. M. Schneerson, *Likutei Sichot* (New York: Kehot Publication Society, 1988), Vol. 26, p. 230.

3. See *Midrash Tanchuma*. Parshat Re'eh chapter 13. The Jerusalem Talmud *Sanhedrin*, chapter 10, Halacha 3. *Yalkut Shimonei, Psalms* chapter 40:37. *Rabbeinu Bachya, Numbers* chapter 16, verse 33. In the name of the Midrash.

4. There are also opinions who assert that *Gehenom* has no physical dimensions whatsoever and, when the Talmud mentions a measurement for *Gehenom* it is only speaking of a spiritual dimension (see *Be'er Hagolah*. Be'er Shishi, Rabbi Yehudah Loew (1512–1609), the Maharal). By this same author, *Tifferet*

the terms fire and water as a metaphor, in order to make the concept more tangible and comprehensive.)

These punishments serve as direct consequences for the soul's actions. If a person sinned on this world with and through fire, for example, rather than using his innate passion and burning love for the service of God, he transgressed and utilized this fiery love for passionate greed, for the love of the materialistic. Then, the method of his purification and refinement must also come through fire. In order to eradicate the unholy fire, we need an opposite fire, a holy fire. Fire is used to fight fire. There is a law in the *Shulchan Aruch* that is as follows:[5] One uses fire to remove dirt ingrained in a pot through fire (i.e., through cooking). Spiritual dirt ingrained with fire must also be removed with fire.

The same holds true when an individual sins with water, meaning coldness. He was cold and indifferent to everything holy and Godly. The purification of this person must also be achieved through coldness. It is common knowledge that when a person is cold and has frostbite, the way to warm him is through rubbing ice on his body.[6] As the talmudic axiom goes, "A person is measured by his own reckoning."[7]

Yisrael (Israel: 1980), chapter 18. See also *The Kuzari* end of Maamor 1. *Emunot VeDeyot*, Maamor 9, chapter 5. *Safer Halkkarim*, Maamor 4, chapter 33. Even according to the opinions mentioned above, which say that it does have a physical dimension, *Gehenom* is a spiritual world with spiritual punishments (or, a refined physical that appears to be spiritual, *Rambam*). (It should be noted that even according to these opinions—*Maharal* etc.—*Gehenom* does exist, it must exist somewhere and that somewhere must be here, for this world is the only creation. The notion that heaven and hell exist somewhere behind the clouds is but a myth. In truth, it exists here, but in a higher spiritual reality.)

5. Rabbi Yoseph Caro, *Shulchan Aruch*. Orach Chayim, chapter 451.
6. See Rabbi Schneur Zalman of Liadi, *Ma'marie Admur Hazaken Enyonim* (New York: Kehot Publication Society, 1983), p. 211.
7. Talmud. *Sotah*, chapter 1, Mishnah 7.

Furthermore, even if one has never sinned while on this earth, he will still need a refinement to shake off the materialistic, so that he can enter the higher spiritual worlds above. This refinement is called *Chibut HaKever*,[8] the pounding of the grave. This means that after the soul departs the body, the body naturally starts to slowly decompose. As the soul of this particular person watches its body deteriorate, it is cause of tremendous pain and grieving for the soul, like a person watching from a distance the home in which he was born and lived his entire life being destroyed by thieves.[9] It is not a physical pain, rather, a tremendous psychological pain and anguish.[10] Needless to say, the quantity of pain the soul experiences will depend on the soul's attachment to its body during its stay on this world. If one was overly engrossed and obsessed with his physical body—and with the material world in general—watching his own body slowly decay could be a most frightening and painful experience. However, a *Tzadik*, who was totally immersed in the spiritual even while on this physical world, might not care as much about his physical decay, for he never really cared about his body even while in this world. Therefore, it says that *Tzadikim* will not be disturbed by *Chibut Ha Kever*.[11]

---

8. Talmud *Berachot* 18b. *Shabbat* 13b and 152b. As explained by Rabbi Saddiah Gaon. *Emunot VeDeyot*, Maamor 6, chapter 7. And Rabbi Menasha Ben Israel. *Nishmat Chayim*, Maamor 2, chapter 24.

9. See Rabbi Saadiah Gaon, *Emunot VeDayot*, Maamor 6, chapter 7.

10. Rabbi Judah HaChassid, *Sefer Chassidim*, Chapter 1163. Rabbi Saadiah Gaon, *Emunot VeDeyot*, Maamor 6, chapter 7. Rabbi Tzvi Hirsh Chayot, *MaHaratz Chayot*. On Talmud *Shabbat* 13b. Rabbi Pinchas Eliyahu Ben Meir of Vilna, *Safer Habrit*, part 2, Maamor 8, chapter 4. Rabbi Menasha Ben Israel, writes that it is like watching a loved one being punished. See *Nishmat Chayim*, Maamor 2, chapter 24.

11. See *Safer Shar HaGilgulim*, Hakdamah 23. It all depends on how much one was attached or detached from the physicality, from the material world. If

There is yet another form of cleansing and refinement that is called *Kaf HaKela*, which is likened to being "thrown by a sling from one end of the world to another."[12]

The explanation of this, is that one of the greatest gifts God bestowed on mankind is the power to forget. The ability to forget is one of the most important ingredients for a healthy human being. Imagine a person possessed of a photographic memory and, consequently, never forgets anything. If this individual goes through very hard and difficult periods in his lifetime and does not have the ability to erase the memory, these terrible travesties experienced will always be before his eyes. This person will never be able to enjoy another true moment of happiness. Consequently, we say it is actually a blessing that we forget; for, we can slowly forget all the hardships we go through (and the same is true the other way around, if we will always be as happy as in the times of our happiest moments, we will never be able to mourn when we must). In order of us to live, we must be able to forget. Forgetting is therefore a necessity for life.[13]

The punishment of *Kaf HaKela* is a punishment of memory. When a soul leaves this physical reality and enters the spiritual worlds above, the first thing it must do, in order to acclimate itself in these spiritual worlds, is forget the physicality. If the soul was a righteous individual during its sojourn on this universe and its physical body—

---

you were totally detached, and were a *Tzadik Gamur* (see *Tanya*, chapter 10), a complete *Tzadik*, and you had zero attachment to physicality, then, there is no need for *Chibut Ha Kever*. (A person who dies *Erev Shabbat* after five o'clock, does not either have this refinement. *Ibid.* Hakdamah 23.)

12. See Talmud. *Shabbat* 152b. *MaHarsha.* Ad loc. *Avot DeRebbe Nathan,* chapter 12. Alluded to in *Samuel* 1, chapter 25, verse 29.

13. See Rabbi Bachya Ibn Pakudah (1050–1120), *Chovot Halevavot* (Diessen: 1946), Shar Habechinah, chapter 5.

and the material world in general—never really had much significance, then the procedure of forgetting the physical will be a very easy and smooth process. In a sense, it was aspiring to forget the physical, its entire life, and remember its true nature. That is, from where and from what lofty levels it came. However, if during its sojourn on this universe, *it forgets about its true—spiritual—reality* and attaches and immerses itself in the physical, its refinement then comes through not allowing it to forget. It is shown the beauty of spiritual worlds above, and at the same time not allowing to forget the lowliness of the physical world (which it now recognizes as low and insignificant). The soul is being thrown from one end of the world—the physical world and desiring it—to another—world of spirituality and desiring it as well.[14] It is like telling someone that he must rejoice at a funeral and weep at a wedding.

In conclusion to the above, we see that punishments for sins are given in *Gehenom*, and reincarnation—in general—is not a form of punishment, rather a process of *Tikkun*—elevation. And the elevation of the soul with all its 613 compartments is done through the 613 *mitzvot*, performed with great care and intensity. If all 613 compartments were not yet elevated, then the soul must return to this lowly world in another human form.[15]

I will digress for a moment and explore in depth these 613 *mitzvot* and their effect on the soul.

---

14. Rabbi Joseph Albo, *Safer Haikkarim*, Maamor 4, chapter 33.
15. See *Safer HaGilgulim*, chapter 4. *Safer Shar HaGilgulim*. Hakdamah 16. *Shulchan Aruch Harov*. Hilchot Talmud Torah, chapter 1, Halacha 4. It should be noted, that in Hakdamah 11 (see also *Shulchan Aruch, Ibid*.), it is stated that one must attempt to study as much all four division of Torah, and if he fails to do so, his soul will have to reincarnate again. From here, it would seem that besides having to be reincarnated for not elevating all 613 parts of the soul

All *mitzvot* are divided into five categories.[16] The first category involves *mitzvot* that can only be performed in a time when the holy Temple is standing, for instance, a sacrifice that can only be offered at the Temple. If an individual is living in a time when these sacrifices are not relevant, it is impossible for him to do this mitzvah and elevate that particular part of his soul. The soul then does not need to reincarnate to elevate that part.[17] However, if one has an express desire to elevate this particular part of his soul, he may do so through learning and studying the laws of the Torah which concern these sacrifices. As the Talmud declares, "One who studies the laws of a sacrifice is considered to have offered that sacrifice."[18]

The second category concerns *mitzvot* that are applicable at all times, in all places. In addition, they are *mitzvot* that "run after" to do; for instance, the *mitzvot* of having faith in God and loving God. If the parts of the soul that are connected with these *mitzvot* were not elevated, the soul will have to reincarnate again to another human being in order for it to be elevated.

The third category of *mitzvot* are those that occur only in certain situations. Therefore, we are *not* in fact obligated to pursue them, only in the event that the situation arises, that is when we must follow through and perform the mitzvah. For instance, the mitzvah of putting a fence on one's

---

(through doing the 613 *mitzvot*), one needs to reincarnate for not studying the complete Torah. Yet this is not the case, for by not studying all four divisions of Torah, one did not thoroughly fulfill the (one) mitzvah of learning Torah. Thus, it is like any other mitzvah, which, if you did not do completely, one needs reincarnation.

16. *Safer Shar HaGilgulim*, Hakdamah 11.
17. *Safer Shar HaGilgulim*, Hakdamah 15.
18. See Talmud. *Menachot* 110a.

rooftop, which means that if a person possesses a home with an open roof, the mitzvah is to make "a fence for the rooftop." If a soul descends until it is totally elevated; yet there remains one mitzvah that it never performed, and that is the mitzvah to make a fence on his rooftop (the reason being that he never owned a home with a rooftop). Then the soul need not reincarnate anymore—it becomes elevated regardless.

However, what happens if the soul is totally elevated and the only mitzvah it did not fulfill is this particular one and it did have the opportunity. Then the soul must return to this world until it performs this final mitzvah. Nonetheless, when this soul will reincarnate, it will surely be a *Tzadik*, a righteous person[19]—like the truly new souls—since the soul is almost completely elevated and is only missing this last mitzvah.

The fourth category involves *mitzvot* that man cannot perform without Divine intervention; for example, that of redeeming one's firstborn male. A person cannot control the gender of his or her first born, this is something only God can control. Therefore, if one's entire soul is elevated and only this category of *mitzvot* is missing, the soul does not then need to reincarnate into another human being. It is sufficient for the soul to descend in an *ibbur*—impregnation (as will be illustrated in the next chapter).

This category, the fifth and final one involves a single mitzvah, that of procreation. This mitzvah is unique in the fact that if a person has elevated his entire soul, and hasn't yet elevated the corresponding part of soul connected with the mitzvah of procreation, then the entire soul—even the

---

19. See *Ibid*. Hakdamah 11.

612 compartments that have already been elevated—has to reincarnate in order to elevate this particular part.[20]

These are the five categories of *mitzvot*. However, there is yet another form of *mitzvot* that does not fall into these categories, and that is *mitzvot* that are given over to a select few. For instance, the mitzvah for a king to write a *Sefer Torah*. The parts of soul that correspond to this mitzvah are elevated through the actions of the king. When the king does these *mitzvot* not only does he elevate his corresponding part of the soul, he actually elevates the entire nation of Israel[21] for his soul is like a general soul in regard to the souls of his subjects. Today, when there are no kings, we can accomplish these *mitzvot* (as we accomplish the *mitzvot* that can only be done in the holy Temple) through studying these laws in the Torah.

Everything discussed until this point has reinforced the idea of reincarnation as a process of *tikkun*/elevation rather than as a form of punishment. Punishment or refinement of the soul occurs in *Gehenom*, as previously discussed.

---

20. And if you are going to ask, if the entire soul has to reincarnate then where is the *you* of the soul, which has to receive its rewards in *Gan Eden* or punishments in *Gehenom*? Moreover, when the time of the resurrection comes along, and the entire soul is now inhabiting another body, how, and with what soul will you be resurrected? This phenomenon is explained in Kabbalah as follows: the you of the soul, the part that goes to *Gan Eden* and the part that will be your soul in the time of resurrection, will not be from your regular soul, rather will be from an early spirit of your soul, a special distinct part of the soul.

21. See Rabbi Schneur Zalman of Liadi, *Tanya* (New York: Kehot Publication Society, 1965), Igerret HaKodesh, 29. Rabbi Pinchas Eliyahu Ben Meir of Vilna, *Safer Habrit* (Jerusalem: Yerid HaSefarim, 1990), part 2, Maamor 3, chapter 2.

Yet, although *Gehenom*, as a purifying and refining mechanism, does "work" excellently for *most* souls; for *Tzadikim*—righteous people, it is not effective. As the Talmud states, "The Fire of *Gehenom* has no dominance over them."[22] The Torah they learned on this world protects them in the worlds above. However, even the greatest of *Tzadikim* sometimes err. As the wisest of men, King Solomon, said, "There is no righteous man on this universe, who does only good and does not sin."[23] (In this instance, sin does not actually mean a literal transgression, rather sin connotes a fault, an incomplete action,[24] for a true *Tzadik* does not ever really transgress.) How can the *Tzaddik* who "sins" be purified in *Gehenom*, if *Gehenom* has no prevalence over him? The Kabbalah answers, "A *Tzadik* who sins must Reincarnate,"[25] and this reincarnation is a form of punishment, to refine the *Tzadik*.

The Kabbalah adds that there is another possible situation in which reincarnation is used as a punishment.[26] When a person does a tremendously grave sin, which is so devastating that no punishment can refine his soul, the punishment then is through reincarnation. The purpose of his soul's next descent will be to elevate and rectify that which he had done in his previous incarnation.

---

22. Talmud. *Chagigah* 27a.
23. *Kohelet*, chapter 7, verse 20.
24. Rashi on *Genesis* chapter 31, verse 39. Rabbi Yehudah Loew, *Nesivat Olam* (Israel: 1980), Nesiv HaTeshuva, chapter 7. Rabbi Yisrael Baal Shem Tov, *Tzavoas Horivash* (New York: Kehot Publication Society, 1982), chapter 133. Rabbi Schneur Zalman of Liadi, *Likkutei Torah* (New York: Kehot Publication Society, 1996), Parshat Mattot, p. 82a. Rabbi M. M. Schneerson, *Safer Hamamarim Meluket* (New York: Kehot Publication Society, 1988), vol. 2, p. 128.
25. *Safer Shar HaGilgulim*, Hakdamah 4 and 22.
26. *Ibid.* Hakdamah 8 and 11, Rabbi Eliyahu ben Moshe Di Viadas, *Reshit Chachmah* (Brooklyn: 1984), Shar Hayira, chapter 13.

When this soul reincarnates the person who contains the soul must elevate it by refraining from committing that particular sin. The question is obvious: How would one know which sin it is that he must be most careful not to transgress?

Rabbi Eliyahu of Vilna, the Vilna Gaon (1720–1797), writes in his commentary to the book of Yonah[27] that a person whose soul descended to purify itself for a particular sin will be able to discern which sin or sins needs purification by examining his nature and finding which sin or sins he feels most naturally inclined to commit. The sin he feels he has the most trouble refraining from and causes him the greatest struggle would be the one that needs purification.[28] In life's journey one encounters difficulty in certain matters. A character trait that one finds difficult to control, such as excessive anger, is one example. This is a sign that the area one is finding challenging may be the very reason one's soul descended upon this earth. Each soul has its own unique purpose and mission. Parallel to the importance and magnitude of a goal are the struggles and challenges in the quest for its accomplishment. What this translates into for our own lives is the ability to welcome and appreciate the challenges which our lives bring us and deal with them as though they were the very reason for our existence. The greater the struggle, the more rewarding the achievement. Such is the outlook of a person attuned to the spirituality in life.[29]

There is yet another form of reincarnation that is a method of punishment, namely reincarnation from one human being

---

27. *The Book of Jonah*, chapter 4, verse 3.
28. Rabbi Moshe Corodovero Shiut Komah (Israel: 1966), chapter 4, p. 166. See also, Rabbi Tzodik HaCohen of Lublin (1823–1900), *Tzidkos Hatzadik*, chapter 49. (See also *Ha'yom Yom*, the 8th day of Nisan.)
29. See Rabbi Yisroel of Modzitz (1848–1920) *Divrei Yisroel* (Israel: 1980), Parshat Bereishit.

to a lower level in creation—from a human being into an animal, a vegetable, or even into an inanimate existence, like sand or stone.[30]

This form of reincarnation is very different from the reincarnation we were discussing until now. In this type of reincarnation, the "you" of the soul, the part of the soul that one has elevated and associated with, is the same part that now reincarnates. Instead of the "you" of the soul going to *Gehenom* to be refined, the "you" descends again down to this lowly world, in order to inhabit a lower creature. Through this incarnation the soul will receive its fitting punishment.

The soul that reincarnates into another human being does so for the purpose of *Tikkun* and therefore becomes the new person's own personal soul. This soul is his Godly soul. It is the soul with which he was born and will die, and the part of this soul that he will elevate will be his forever. However, by a reincarnation from a human into a lower being, the soul goes into an existing creation, which already has its own soul, and this punished soul does not animate the being, it merely resides within it and suffers.[31]

What is the reason for this form of punishment? Why would a person deserve this sort of suffering and how does this serve as a purification?

---

30. *Safer Hakana.* (Attributed to Rabbi Nachunya ben Hakana, a first century saint.) Sod Ve'onesh Gilgul Al Ha'arayot (Israel: 1973), p. 192. Rabbi Yoseph Caro, *Magid Mesharim* (Jerusalem: Orah, 1960), Parshat Vayikra, p. 87. Rabbi Eliezer Ezcary. *Safer Cheraidim*, chapter 33. Rabbi Meir Ben Gabbai. *Avodat Hakodesh* part 2, chapter 34. Rabbi Avraham Azulay. *Chesed LeAvraham*, part 2, chapter 47. Rabbi Menasha Ben Israel. *Nishmat Chayim* Maamor 4, chapter 13. Rabbi Pinchas Eliyahu Ben Meir of Vilna. *Safer Habrit* part 2, Maamor 8, chapter 2. Rabbi Chaim Ibn Attar (1696–1743) *Or HaChaim Genesis* chapter 1, verse 26.

31. See Safer HaGilgulim. Hakdamah 22. See also, The commentary *Benei Aharon*. Ad loc.

The soul descends to this world in order to elevate the physical. This is done through taking a tangible, material object and elevating it to holiness by using it for a mitzvah, thereupon elevating the Godly sparks that reside in all physical matter.

As explained in the Kabbalah,[32] every single existence on this earth, from the highest of creatures—humans—to the inanimate, contains a Godly spark. And the purpose for man's creation is so that he should elevate all these sparks to their original source in holiness.

An example of how this is done: a person takes a kosher animal and slaughters it according to *halacha* and then eats the meat with the intention of using the strength from its nutrients to help him serve God. The meat then becomes elevated from its animal state to a state of holiness. However, it should be noted that according to the Kabbalah,[33] if a person eats meat and does not have any Godly intentions, he just eats to sate his hunger, then there is no elevation at all—not only is the meat not elevated to Godliness, he does not even elevate it to the level of man. Thereupon, the Talmud states, "An unlearned person should not meat."[34] A person who will only eat the meat to feed his own hunger should refrain from eating it, for he does not accomplish any form of elevation through the consumption of the food; and without this elevation, he is no better than the animal that he eats. Nevertheless, he is permitted to eat from the vegetable kingdom, for man must eat to survive.

This process of elevation is done through every *positive* commandment that we do. How does one elevate, however,

---

32. *Ibid.*
33. *Safer HaGilgulim,* Sader HaGilgulim.
34. Talmud. *Pesachim* 49b.

that which the Torah forbids us? Just as there is elevation through positive action, there is also elevation through the negative "nonactions." This is elevation through *Dichiyah*, avoidance or resistance. Through avoiding and withdrawing from these unholy entities, one elevates them.

Just as there is the ability to elevate that which is low, conversely, one can lower himself to the level of that with which he has contact. Man, the rational animal, an intellectual being, should be dictated by his intelligence. Nevertheless, man has the choice to act—if he so desires— like an animal, to be directed by his animalistic soul, and thus to act instinctively rather than intellectually, to be led by pure emotion. As previously mentioned, a human being's natural instincts or animalistic soul are not necessarily bad or evil. They are selfish and egotistic and are the basic survival instincts. However, these instincts can potentially lead a person to actual evil; for example, in order to survive, he may feel the need to commit a crime. The Midrash states, "The wicked are enslaved by their Emotions."[35] Their intellect is controlled by their feelings; their minds are in the possession of their hearts. Furthermore, a human being has the choice to lower himself even further, to decend to the level of an inanimate, inorganic being. He can choose to behave like a stone, to be totally cold and indifferent, with no emotions, regarding holiness. Just as all punishments are a direct consequence of a person's actions, so it is with these punishments. If one has lowered himself and acted as an animal, then his refinement comes through reincarnating into a animal. If one behaved like a stone, then this individual will have to reincarnate into a stone.

---

35. *Midrash Rabbah*. Genesis Parshah 34, chapter 11.

The chassidic Rebbe, Rabbi Pinchas of Koritz (1728–1791), once said in jest,[36] that a conceited person will be reincarnated in a buzzing bee[37] because this person continuously says, "I am this": and "I am that." In Yiddish, he would be saying, "*Ich Bin, Ich Bin.*" *Bin* is the Yiddish word for bee. Therefore, says Reb Pinchas, since he is always saying "*Ich Bin,*" which in Yiddish translates into, "I Am a Bee," thus he will finally become—through reincarnation—a bee.

These reincarnations are a tremendous punishment for the soul, because of the immense pain the soul suffers while being reincarnated in the animal or the inanimate. The soul suffers psychologically, it is embarrassed at being a human soul now in the form of an animal or a lower creature. The analogy given is of a wise man who sinned and, as a form of punishment, was bound with chains to a fool, so he would share with the fool all of life's experiences.[38] In addition to this psychological pain, there is also a real, tangible pain that the soul endures (as much as is possible in regards to spiritual entity).

The suffering of the human soul trapped within a lower being is tremendous. It is the pain of a confinement which limits one's ability to express themselves. To fully comprehend and appreciate the depth of this refinement, we must understand the "construction" of the soul and the very nature of the soul itself.

---

36. "Midrash Pinchas" (Jerusalem: 1971), p. 81, chapter 35.

37. The reason why a conceited person, one who only thinks about himself, reincarnates in a buzzing bee, is explained, because a bee is the exact antithesis of conceit. A bee by nature never thinks for himself. All his actions are done for the benefit of the entire hive. See Rabbi Avraham Azulay (1570–1643), *Chesed Le'Avraham* (Jerusalem, Ben Yishai, 1997), part 5, chapter 24.

38. A parable given by Rabbi Menasha Ben Israel. *Nishmat Chayim*, Maamor 4, chapter 13.

We speak of the soul's intelligence, emotions, desires, and so on. However, this is not the essence of the soul; it is only a manifestation of what the soul actually is. Nevertheless, the manifestations that come forth from the essence do have an existence in the essence of the soul, even before they manifest themselves, although in the essence they are not yet revealed. Therefore, in order for these manifestations of the soul to reveal themselves, they need their fitting vessels, they need the appropriate *Keilim*. The physical shape of the human body fits the spiritual shape of the soul and, therefore, enables it to express itself.[39]

The Torah states,[40] "For my Nation is truly a part of God." Just as the name of God (the Tetragrammaton) is divided into four letters, the first letter being the *Yud* (י) then the *Hei* (ה) the *Vov* (ו) and then another *Hei* (ה), the same is true with the soul of man. It is generally divided into four compartments.[41] The Yud—which is just a small dot—represents in man the level of *Chochmah*—wisdom, the intuition of thoughts, for when the thought first enters the mind, it is but a small dot (it is not yet a fully understood thought; it does not extend). The next letter is the *Hei*, which is a broader and more spacious letter. It extends longer and is wider. This represents in man the level of *Binah*—understanding. The thought in this level becomes formulated into comprehensive thoughts, and it increases in its width and breadth. The third letter, the letter *Vov*, represents the attribute of emotion. The soul's emotions are derived from intellect. The thought is internalized, it is brought down to one's level, similar to the letter *Vov*, which

---

39. See Rabbi Hayim Vital, *Sharrei Kedushah*, part 1, Shar 1.
40. *Deuteronomy*, chapter 32, verse 9.
41. Rabbi Schneur Zalman of Liadi, *Tanya* (New York:Kehot Publication Society, 1965), *Igeret HaTeshuva*, chapter 4.

has only length, representing the idea of taking from the above and drawing it down below. The last letter, the *Hei*, is once again a letter with a width and a breadth; thus, it represents in man the level of *Malchut*—sovereignty, dominance, expanding one's majestic influence to the width and breadth.

Just as the four letters of God's name correspond to the four divisions of soul, they also correspond with the physical structure of the body. The human body is divided into four parts.[42] The head of the human being corresponds to the letter *Yud* (the dot above). The length of the human body corresponds to the letter *Vov* (a long letter). The five fingers of man correspond to the letter *Hei* (for *Hei* is number five in the Hebrew counting). And the five toes of man correspond to the second letter *Hei*. Thus, the body of a human being was meant and created to fit the human soul.

Moreover, it is explained[43] that even the specific levels of soul have their unique place whence they manifest themselves in the body, for instance, even the various divisions of intelligence have their distinct location in the physical brain: *Chochmah*—wisdom, intuition, or intuitive thoughts —and *Binah*—understanding, formulating, and comprehending the thoughts. There is a part of the brain for the level of *Chochmah*, and there is another part for *Binah*.

Every physical creation in this world has two elements.[44]

---

42. Rabbi Yoseph Yitzchak, the sixth Chabad Rebbe. *Safer HaMaamorim 5708* (New York: Kehot Publication Society, 1958), VaYetzer Hashem, p. 66. The Lubavitcher Rebbe, *Sefer HaMaamorim Meluket* (New York: Kehot Publication Society, 1993), vol. 4, p. 274.

43. *Zohar* part 3, pp. 136, 146. Rabbi Yoseph Yitzchak, the sixth Chabad Rebbe. *Safer HaMaamorim 5700* (New York: Kehot Publication Society, 1962), Lecha Amar, p. 164.

44. Rabbi Yoseph Yitzchak, the sixth Chabad Rebbe. *Safer HaMaamorim 5710* (New York: Kehot Publication Society, 1951), Ki Chak LeYisrael, p. 13.

The actual existence: the mere fact that it exists; and its specific shape and form, which God creates for the existence. Chassidus explains that, in a sense, the shape and form of every existence brings about its *Bittul*—nullification of self, namely, its ability to recognize Godliness. Its actual existence (*Yesh*), seems to have occurred on its own, without Divine intervention. But in recognizing its very own physical shape and form, which is direcly analogous to its soul, that which animates and gives it life, it realizes its soul, and through the recognition of the soul one realizes his true source.

And now we can begin to understand the immense pain of the soul within a lower being. To the essence of the soul, it makes no difference whence it is located;[45] even in the body of a human it does not express itself, it just exists. However, the part of the soul that expresses itself, be it through intellect or emotion, suffers tremendously when it inhabits a being in which it cannot properly express its qualities. The nature of the soul is to reveal itself, and this punishment is contrary to its very nature. It is as if one would take a free man, and put him away in a prison, trapped and unable to free himself.

When the soul resides in an animal, it does have limited room for expression, for an animal does have some form of intelligence and emotion. However, when the soul reincarnates into an inanimate creation—for example, a stone—the suffering is enormous for it has no outlet for expression, the stone has neither intelligence nor emotion. Accordingly, it is understood that the lower the soul reincarnates, the greater its pain.

---

45. Rabbi Schneur Zalman of Liadi, *Sidur Eim Dach* (New York:Kehot Publication Society, 1965), p. 48. See also, Rabbi Shmuel, the fifth Chabad Rebbe, *Safer HaMaamorim 5630* (New York: Kehot Publication Society, 1980), p. 292.

It must be reiterated, however, that this is not an act of revenge on God's part. It is a process of cleansing and, therefore, an act of kindness on the part of God. The esteemed rabbi of seventeenth century Amsterdam, Rabbi Menashe Ben Israel, writes[46] that the word *gilgul* (גלגול) in Hebrew letters equals in numerical value the Hebrew word for kindness, which is *chesed*. This implies that reincarnations are actually a kindess.[47]

The length of time that the soul spends in the lower being depends on the sin for which it is being cleansed. If the lower being that it is inhabiting happens to die during its sentence, the soul will be transplanted into another live animal.[48]

After the soul has completed its sentence within the lower being, it still has not completed all of its elevations (unless it was within the animal kingdom). If the soul was in an inanimate being, it must still go into the vegetable kingdom and then the animal kingdom, and only then has it completed its elevations and so on. (It can only elevate one level at a time, and it must elevate past all three kingdoms.[49])

Furthermore, there is also a particular time of the year when each one of these levels can be elevated. For example, if the soul was reincarnated into an inanimate creation and the punishment was for a period of five years, after the pe-

---

46. See *Nishmat Hayim*, Maamor 4, chapter 16. This numerical equation is also recorded by Rabbi Yeshayah Halevi Horowitz, *Shalah HoKodesh*. Shnei Luchot Habrit (Jerusalem: 1963), *Safer Bamidbar Devarim Re'eh Torah Or* 7. Rabbi Nathan Shapiro (1585–1633) *Megalah Amukhot* chapter 11. Rabbi Naphtali Hirtz Bacharach, *Emek HaMelech*. Hakdamah 2, chapter 3.
47. See Rabbi Meir Ben Gabbai, *Avodat Hakodesh* part 2, chapters 32, 33. Rabbi Dan Yitzchak Arbarbanel, *Deuteronomy*, Parshat Teitzei.
48. See *Safer Shar HaGilgulim*, Hakdamah 22.
49. See *Ibid.*

riod of five years *to date* (when the five years terminate), the soul will not automatically be elevated to the level of vegetative, because there are particular months in the year when souls inhabiting the inanimate are elevated from those levels. And, there are special months of the year when souls are elevated from the level of vegetative, and there are times of elevation for souls in the animal kingdom.

The year, which has twelve months, is divided into three divisions: the first four months, the middle four months, and the last four months. Therefore, if (for example) a soul descended into a stone in the first month of the year, in the month of Nisan, for five years, thus after the five years, the soul must wait awhile (another four months) until the middle four months of the year, for these are the months when souls ascend from the inanimate. And if the soul reincarnated into a vegetable for a period of five years, in the sixth month of Elul, then after five years, the soul will have to wait until the first four months of the year. Thus, the soul will have to wait yet another six months until the first of the first four months to be elevated. And likewise, if the soul was reincarnated into an animal in the first month of the year, in the month of Nissan for a period of five years, after five years, the soul will have to wait another eight months until the first of the last four months of the year.[50]

All these elevations will occur automatically, in their set time. However, with man's intervention, the time of the sentence can be shortened. If a human being eats an animal that contains within it a human soul, he can then elevate the soul even before the time that was set for its cleansing period.

Moreover, if there is a soul within a vegetation, and a person consumes it, not only can he elevate the soul before

---

50. See *Ibid.*

its set time, he can even elevate the soul two levels at a time. Through eating this vegetation, he elevates the soul from the level of vegetative to the level of humans, skipping over the level of animals. And if by chance, in the vegetation, there happened to be a speck of sand (the inanimate) that contained within it a human soul, then he can elevate the soul imprisoned in the sand, all three levels at once, from inorganic to human.[51] However, in the Kabbalah,[52] it states clearly that in order to elevate the soul of one who is reincarnated into a lower creature, the person eating the food must have some sort of connection with the soul he is consuming. They both must share the same root of soul, they both must stem from the same area in the general soul of Adam.

If a person desires to elevate the human soul contained within the food, he must consume the food with higher intentions, *Kavanah*, namely the intention that, through eating this physical nourishment which one's body requires, one will then have a healthy body with which to serve God. If, however, the person consumed a piece of bread with a soul of a human contained in it and had no intentions, then although an elevation of the soul did occur, it was not a positive elevation. On the contrary, it was negative, for the soul that was in this food is now elevated to the level of man in a negative sense. Therefore, it causes only problems, and, furthermore, can harm the 'eater' spiritually.[53] Therefore, the Talmud declares, "An unlearned person should not eat

---

51. See *Ibid.*
52. *Safer Hagilgulim*. Sader Gilgulim, chapter 4.
53. *Safer HaGilgulim*, Sader Gilgulim, chapter 4. See also: Rabbi Moshe Corodovero Shiur Komah (Israel: 1966) chapter 4, p. 168.

meat."[54] However, there is no ruling against eating vegetables, although it is possible that there would be a human soul in it.[55]

These elevations that occur before the soul's set time can also be accomplished by animals themselves.[56] If an animal eats a vegetable containing within it a human soul, the animal can then elevate the soul to the level of the animal kingdom. Although the animal does not consume the vegetable with a Godly intention, nevertheless, animals have no free will and thus everything they do is a direct manifestation of the will of God, for they have no other will, and therefore, their eating can also elevate.

Only the most extreme sinners, those who have committed the most terrible sins, are punished through reincarnation into a lower being. Reb Hayim Vital states that, when these sinners die, they first enter *Gehenom*, but it is not enough to cleanse them of their sins; and therefore, they must go down into lower beings.[57] Moreover, there are sinners, who are not even meritorious enough to enter *Gehenom* (which is a much lighter punishment). These souls return to this lowly world immediately following their deaths, and through their reincarnations here below, they receive their appropriate refinements, until eventually they too are able

---

54. Talmud. *Pesachim* 49b. However, on the Holy day of Shabbat everyone may eat meat, for on Shabbat everyone receives an extra soul, that assists with the elevation.

55. In *Safer HaGilgulim*, Sader Gilgulim, chapter 4, it is written, that the reason why the unlearned can eat vegetables, is, because they have not sinned so harshly to punish them so severely.

56. See *Safer Shar HaGilgulim*, Hakdam 22. Rabbi Avraham Azulay, *Chesed LeAvraham* part 5, chapter 24.

57. *Safer Shar HaGilgulim*, Hakdam 22. See also, *Reshit Chachmah*. Shar HaYirah, chapter 13.

to gain entry into *Gan Eden*. Even the greatest of sinners inevitably enters Paradise. As the Prophet says, "His banished will not be rejected by Him."[58] Even if it takes one or more reincarnations until the soul is worthy enough to enter Paradise,[59] eventually all souls will enter.

Gehenom has no effect on the extreme sinners, and conversely, it has no effect on a great *Tzadik* as well, albeit for the opposite reasons. Since *Tzadikim* cannot be affected by *Gehenom*, if they are in need of purification, they must go down into a lower being as well, for a short period of time, and to a higher level of creation. It says in Kabbalah that *Tzadikim* reincarnate into fish.[60]

In summary, there are two major forms of reincarnation. The first being reincarnation from one human being to another for the purpose of *Tikkun*. (This reincarnation applies to most people, for there are few people—if any—who can elevate all three divisions of the soul, with all 613 subdivisions.) The second form of reincarnation is reincarnation as a form of punishment and refinement. This sort of reincarnation is from a human being into a lower creation. Most souls do not reincar-

---

58. *Samuel* II chapter 14, verse 14.
59. Rabbi Schneur Zalman of Liadi, *Tanya* (New York: Kehot Publication Society, 1965), end of chapter 39.
60. *Safer Shar HaGilgulim*, Hakdamah 4. See Rabbi Shneur Zalman of Liadi. *Meah Sh'arim* (New York: Kehot Publication Society, 1967), p. 33. For the reason why *Tzadikim* reincarnate into fish, see Rabbi Chaim Ibn Attar (1696–1743) *Or HaChaim. Genesis* chapter 1, verse 26, and Rabbi Tzvi Elimelech (Shapira) of Dinov (1785–1841) *Bnei Yissaschar* (Bnei Brak: Heichel HaSafer), Maamorei Chodesh Sivan, Maamor 5 writes that the reason why reincarnation in fish is the lightest possible punishment of all reincarnations, is because, according to Jewish law, fish do not need to be ritually slaughtered before being eaten. Thus, the pain they (the souls inhabiting these fish) suffer through death, is far less severe. See also: Rabbi Yonathan Eibeschuretz Yarot D'Vash (Jerusalem: Levin-Epstain), part 1, p. 10A.

nate in such a fashion. It only applies to either a great *Tzadik*, on whom *Gehenom* has no bearing, or a great sinner for whom *Gehenom* is not enough.

"The power of *teshuva* is such that its reach is far beyond that of the cleansing through reincarnation." The potential to cleanse through reincarnation is truly great; yet, it pales in comparison to the awesome strength of *teshuva*. Through a true sigh of remorse, a person returns to his true source of holiness and erases all negativity, accomplishing more than centuries of reincarnations.[61]

In addition to the two main forms of reincarnation, there are other instances that necessitate reincarnation.

There is another form of reincarnation into humans that is not for *Tikkun*, nor punishment. This form of reincarnation occurs when one's soul reincarnates for the purpose of helping another human reach his proper elevation.

This kind of reincarnation takes place with a soul that completed all the elevations (*Tikkun*) necessary for its entire *Nefesh*, *Ruach*, and *Neshamah*. It reincarnates to assist and guide another un-elevated soul whose soul comes from the same source as the elevated soul (e.g., they both are from the general soul of Adam and from within that general soul, they both stem from the hands of Adam). The reason this soul reincarnates to help another un-elevated soul is that they share the same roots of soul within the general soul of Adam, and, therefore, are responsible for one another.[62]

---

61. Rabbi Avraham Azulay, *Chesed LeAvraham*, part 1, chapter 12. See also: Rabbi Moshe Corodovero *Shiur Komah* (Israel: 1966), chapter 4, p. 168.

62. Although the Talmud states, *Shevuot* 39, "All Jews are interlinked," nevertheless there is a difference to what extent, for there are some souls, who are more connected than others.

There is a soul that is called the "universal soul."[63] This soul is connected to all souls, and can also reincarnate solely for the purpose of helping other souls achieve their proper elevation. A universal soul has the responsibility for all souls, being that it is connected with all souls.[64] When this "universal soul" reincarnates to help other people reach ther elevations, it is guaranteed that this elevated soul will not sin and will be inclined to do only good. Furthermore, this "universal soul" can attain all three levels of soul very easily, even at a very young age, while a child.[65] This phenomenon is called in the Kabbalah[66] a "*Yinukah,*" a spiritual prodigy.

There is yet another cause for reincarnation into another human being, and that is reincarnation for one's spouse.[67] If for instance, a man must reincarnate owing to the unelevated status of his soul, but his wife has already completely elevated her soul, then, assuming the husband has a significant "*Zecut*"—merit, the soul of his wife will reincarnate with him, in order to live with her husband, her true soul mate.

An interesting phenomenon discussed in kabbalistic literature is the descent of multiple souls that merge and form a unified soul within a single person. Moreover, each

---

63. Rabbi Schneur Zalman of Liadi. *Tanya* (New York: Kehot Publication Society, 1965), chapters 2 and 42.
64. See Rabbi Menachem Mendel, the third Chabad Rebbe, *Derech Mitzvotecha*. Mitzvat Ahavat Yisrael (New York: Kehot Publication Society, 1953), p. 56, where it is written that the reason why it says (see *Taamei Hamitzvot of the Ari Zal,* Parshat Kedoshim) that the Holy Ari Zal recited the prayer of penitence daily (although he surely did not sin) was because his soul was a general soul. A soul who feels all other souls, and thus repents for them.
65. *Safer Shar HaGilgulim,* Hakdamah 7 and 8.
66. See *Ibid. Zohar,* Parshat Balak.
67. *Safer Shar HaGilgulim,* Hakdamah 8.

of these souls may have a different purpose, a unique reason for reincarnating.

Rabbi Hayim Vital writes[68] that his own soul is a composite of three souls of *Tzadikim*, who sinned (at their level) and, thus, had to be reincarnated again to receive their appropriate punishments.

Yet, he writes of himself elsewhere,[69] that his soul is a new soul, descended to this world for the very first time.

When Rabbi Vital speaks of his 'new soul' he is really referring to his unique personality, the "you of the soul." That is the part of the soul with which he associated and connected. This soul was a soul that never yet came down to this world. However, along with his soul at the time of his birth came the departed souls of three *Tzadikim*. They connected themselves with Reb Hayim's new soul and descended to this world in order to receive their appropriate punishments.

Thus, while his distinct soul descended to this world for the purpose of elevation (*Tikkun*), the souls of these three *Tzadikim* descended for the purpose of purification.

Just as it is a terrible punishment for a human soul to reincarnate into a lower creature, because the soul cannot express and reveal itself, the same is true regarding human souls reincarnated into other humans souls, because these souls, these previous personalities of the three *Tzadikim*[70] are now reincarnated into another being, another personality that reveals and expresses its own unique soul, its unique traits. Consequently, these three souls are now im-

---

68. See *Ibid.*
69. See *Ibid.*
70. *Ibid.* Three souls can be reincarnated into one body.

prisoned, for they cannot express their own personalities, their traits.

A soul that reincarnates into a human as a punishment must have a connection with the soul of the human whom it inhabits, namely, they must stem from the same source in the general soul of Adam.[71]

---

71. See *Ibid.* Hakdamah 5 and 38.

5
Different Forms of Reincarnation: *Ibbur* and Dybbuk

There is another form of reincarnation that is termed in the Kabbalah,[1] "Gilgul Kaful"—"double reincarnation." The Kabbalah explains that this refers to a *Tzadik* who had completely elevated his entire soul; yet, he had committed a minor sin. The "you" of his soul will then have to be reincarnated into another human being so that he can correct and rectify his sin.

However, this form of reincarnation is vastly different from the reincarnations mentioned in the previous chapter. In the previous chapter, we spoke of three souls of *Tzadikim* reincarnated into the soul of Rabbi Hayim Vital. The difference between that form of reincarnation and "double reincarnation" is that, in the case of Rabbi Hayim, all four souls

---

1. *Safer Shar Hagilgulim*, Hakdamah 11. Rabbi Avraham Azulay writes that there can be an *ibbur*, even from a *Ruach*, spirit, of our forefathers Avraham, Yitzchak, and Yakov. See *Chesed LeAvraham*, part 5, chapter 20. See also Rabbi Menasha Ben Israel, *Nishmat Chayim*. Maamor 4, chapter 12.

including his own, formed one collective soul. However, in this case, the soul of the *Tzadik* who is reincarnated will never become part of the person's soul; his soul will be like a "visiting guest." After this soul achieves its appropriate purification, the soul will exit the body to enter *Gan Eden*. However, the three souls of the *Tzadikim* within Reb Hayim were required to stay within him throughout his entire life span. They did not have the option of leaving for they were all one single unified soul.

Both of these scenarios are termed reincarnation. By definition, reincarnation (between humans) requires the soul to be present in the body it reincarnates into at the time of birth.

Within the general topic of the soul's journey, is the concept of *ibbur* (impregnation). Just as a pregnant woman has a new existence added to her own being, the same is true with these types of "reincarnations." It is possible that during one's lifetime, the soul of another human being will be impregnated into one's own soul. A soul will be added to his existence; a soul that was not born together with him will descend into his soul.[2] (According to Kabbalah, *ibbur* can only occur at the age of maturity, which is age 13 for boys and 12 for girls.[3])

There are generally two types of *ibbur*. One is when the soul which impregnates does it to assist the person he descends into. For example, a person with an ordinary 'new soul' has already elevated his entire level of *Nefesh*, and now must attain the higher levels of soul through great difficulties (or through *Yibum*). He stands on the threshold, yet has not yet attained the new level of soul; the soul of an elevated

---

2. See *Ibid*. Numerous places, for instance Hakdamahs 1, 2, and 3.
3. *Ibid*. Hakdamah 38.

Tzadik will then descend below to be impregnated into him, until his soul becomes like the soul of that *Tzadik*.[4]

In accordance with this concept, Rabbi Schneur Zalman (the first Chabad Rebbe) answers the famous paradox in *Tanya*.[5] Before a soul descends below, God makes it swear that it will be a *Tzadik*.[6] However, this seems to contradict the saying, "You, God, have created the righteous."[7] (Namely, there are special souls created to be *Tzadikim*![8]) The Rebbe explains, that through hard and strenuous toil, it is possible for the soul of a departed *Tzadik* to come down below and be impregnated into him, upon which time he can become—just as he swore before his birth—a *Tzadik*.

The above-mentioned refers to the first type of *ibbur*. The second type of *ibbur* concerns a person who excels in a particular mitzvah and performs it with tremendous caution and vigilance. It is possible for the soul of a *Tzadik* whom, during his lifetime, excelled in this same area, to impregnate this person's soul, even before this person finishes elevating his entire *Nefesh*.

Furthermore, it is feasible that a *Tzadik* who is still alive will become impregnated into another living human being. They are both alive, and yet at the same time, the soul of one living human being—the *Tzadik*—becomes impregnated into another living human being.[9] As the Torah says, regarding

---

4. *Ibid.* Hakdamah 2.
5. See, Rabbi Schneur Zalman of Liadi, *Tanya* (New York: Kehot Publication Society, 1965), chapter 1 for the question and chapter 14 for the response.
6. Talmud. *Nidah* 30b.
7. See Talmud. *Bava Batrah* 16a.
8. Rabbi Schneur Zalman of Liadi, *Tanya* (New York: Kehot Publication Society, 1965), chapter 14.
9. *Safer Shar HaGilgulim*, Hakdamah 3. Rabbi Avraham Azulay, *Chesed LeAvraham*, part 5, chapter 20.

King David's love for Jonathan, "And Jonathan's soul joined with the soul of David,"[10] which the Kabbalah explains to mean that the souls of these friends were literally joined as one.[11] David's soul while still alive was impregnated into the soul of his beloved friend Jonathan, and they became one.

Although it is possible for the soul of a living *Tzadik* to impregnate another living person, the part of the soul which impregnates is not the actual soul of the *Tzadik*, it is only a spirit and shadow of his soul.[12]

It is also possible for a person to experience an *ibbur* from his own soul. This means that if a person is worthy enough and deserves spiritual assistance, then the parts of his soul that were already elevated in previous lifetimes, can now be impregnated his soul, in order to assist with the elevation of his soul.[13] It is possible for the 'positive' of his previous reincarnations to descend into his soul to help him achieve his elevations.[14] Positive, meaning the elevated compartments of his soul.

In all these levels of *ibbur*, the soul that becomes impregnated experiences the following:

1. It is like a guest in the body it inhabits and, therefore, can come and go in and out of the body as it pleases. It is not bound to the body.

---

10. *Samuel* 1, chapter 18, verse 1.
11. See The Commentary, by Rabbi Yechiel Hilel Ben David, *Mitzudot Tzion*. Ad loc.
12. *Safer Shar HaGilgulim*, Hakdamah 1.
13. See *Ibid*. Hakdamah 3.
14. Rabbi M. M. Schneerson. *Likutei Sichot* (New York: Kehot Publication Society, 1964), Vol. 1, p. 67.

2. It does not experience any pain or discomfort from inhabiting the body (as opposed to the pain experienced with *gilgul*).
3. It can only gain spiritually from inhabiting the body. This means that it only attains the rewards and not the punishments.[15] This is because this soul inhabits the body only to do good, to assist with the elevation. Thus, when he feels that, by inhabiting this body, his spirituality might be affected, he immediately leaves the body.

The above-mentioned forms of *ibbur* were for the assistance of the person the soul entered. There is another form of *ibbur* that is a punishment. For example, a *Tzadik* who only committed a single minor sin during his lifetime needs to be purified and refined, yet the punishments of *Gehenom* have no effect on his soul. In this case, it is possible for this soul to become impregnated into another existing human being. Nevertheless, this is not called *gilgul* (reincarnation); it is called *ibbur* (impregnation). *Gilgul*, by definition, means that the reincarnated soul is born together with the body.

However, in the above-mentioned scenario, *ibbur* is a form of punishment for the *Tzadik*, the soul is not like a guest. It cannot come and go as it pleases, and it feels all the pain suffered by the body it inhabits.[16]

In all these forms of *ibbur*, the souls that co-exist are connected and originate from the same source in the general soul of Adam.

---

15. *Safer Shar HaGilgulim*, Hakdamah 2 and 3.
16. *Ibid*. Hakdamah 5. See *Benie Aharon*, number 1, for a lengthy explanation of this concept.

There is *ibbur* to assist the soul in a positive way, yet, *ibbur* has the potential to cause spiritual problems as well. For example, a person who is a sinner may be impregnated with a soul of a departed sinner for whom *Gehenom* was not punishment enough. This soul will impregnate into his body and cause him to experience spiritual difficulties.[17]

In order for two souls to co-exist within a being, there must be a third soul which unites them.[18] Hence, this person now has three souls inhabiting his body: his soul, the soul of the departed *Tzadik* (or his own previously elevated parts), and the third soul that unites them both. With three souls, it is understood that this person can now attain great spiritual levels. Moreover, the Kabbalah says[19] that this third soul has to be a very lofty soul. It has to be a soul that never yet descended down to this lowly world. Furthermore, the Kabbalah states, one actually needs a fourth soul to oversee and make sure the third soul does what it has to accomplish.[20]

We spoke of *ibbur* as a form of punishment for slight imperfections that do not require a full reincarnation, yet must be refined. There is a documented case of this kind of *ibbur* that involves ten great talmudic sages in the second century. In the prayers on Yom Kippur,[21] we tell their story. There were ten talmudic sages who were brutally murdered to rectify and purify the souls of the ten sons of Jacob who sold their brother Yoseph as a slave.[22] It is

---
17. Ibid. Hakdamah 22.
18. Ibid. Hakdamah 32.
19. Ibid.
20. Ibid.
21. See The famous prayer titled, *Tiher Rabbi Ishmael*.
22. Midrash *Beit HaMidrash* 5:176. See *Zohar Chadash*, p. 100. See also *Zohar Chadash*, p. 96.

stated[23] that these ten sages possessed the souls of the ten sons of Jacob. From this we may infer that the ten sages were reincarnations of the ten souls and received their purification through their terrible deaths. However, this assumption creates a paradox.

In the Zohar it states clearly,[24] "one should never say that the holy sons of Jacob were deserving of any form of punishment, and, even if they had sinned, they surely did the proper *teshuva*, repentance, while on this earth and were definitely not deserving of reincarnation as a punishment."

So, how can we reconcile these two opposing statements of the kabbalah? Did they need to be reincarnated to receive a punishment or not?[25]

The Kabbalah resolves this seeming incongruity by explaining[26] that, in truth, the souls of the ten sons of Jacob were not reincarnated into these ten sages, rather, they were impregnated into their souls.[27] Thus, the ten sons suffered

---

23. See *Safer Shar HaGilgulim*, in numerous places, for instance, Hakdamah 39. Rabbi Yitzchak of Acco, *Meirat Einayim*, Parshat Bereishit 4:1. *Rabbeinu Bachya*. Genesis chapter 44, verse 17. Rabbi Yeshayah Halevi Horowitz, *Shallah HaKodesh*, Shnei Luchot Habbrit. Parshat Vayeshev Mikketz Vayigash Torah Or 1. Rabbi Shem Tov Ben Shem Tov Safer ha'eMunot (Jerusalem: 1969) Shar 7, chapter 8. Furthermore, the kabbalists point out, the numerical volume of the ten sons of Yakov (excluding Yoseph and Binyamin) equals two thousand eight hundred fifty eight—as the numerical volume of the ten saints. Rabbi Menachem, *Recanti*. Genesis. Parshat Vayeshev. Rabbi Menasha Ben Israel. *Nishmat Chayim*. Maamor, 4, chapter 10.
24. *Tikkunei Zohar*. Tikkun 29, p. 110.
25. *Safer HaGigulim*. Sader Gilgulim, chapter 15.
26. *Safer Shar HaGilgulim*. Hakdamah 39.
27. See: Rabbi Jonathan Eibeschuetz (1690–1764), *Tifferet Yihonoton*. Parshat Mikketz, where it seems suggested from the moment of his writings, about the reincarnations of the ten tribes that it was not a regular form of reincarnation—where the reincarnated soul becomes the second person's soul—rather more like an *ibbur*, where the soul can depart from the body it now

only slightly through the sages' deaths, and fulfilled the purpose of their descent, namely their souls' refinement and elevation, from its slight imperfection.

As mentioned previously, the difference between *gilgul* and *ibbur* is that reincarnations—*gilgul*, are from the time of birth, while impregnation—*ibbur*, can occur many years after one's birth.

This is how they differ; yet, they are similar in that once all these souls unite in one body, they form one unified soul.[28] Even though the soul impregnates into an existing body and can come and go as it pleases, while it resides within the person, it unites with his other soul and becomes a part of him, so much so that he might not even feel that he has an extra soul. Even if he *does* feel the extra soul, it doesn't feel like an invasion into his body. It feels as though it is a part of him.

There is an ancient custom[29] which is practiced the day before Yom Kippur. Every person takes a live animal (usually a fish or a chicken) as an atonement for the sins they committed. This is called *Kaporot*. The law in regard to a pregnant woman is that she should take an extra chicken as an atonement for the unborn child she is carrying.[30] Yet the child is not yet born and does not even have a separate existence. What sins can it commit in its mother's womb? Why does it need an atonement?

---

inhabits. See also Rabbi Shem Tov Ben Shem Tov *Safer Ha'eMunot* (Jerusalem 1969), Shar 7, chapter 8.

28. It should be noted, that it states in *Safer Shar HaGilgulim* (for example, Hakdamah 32) that there are souls who are a synthesis of many different souls. For instance, the soul of Pinchat is a combination that the souls of Yoseph and Yitro.

29. Dating back to the times of the Gaonim. See *Otzar HaGaonim*, Yuma pp. 62, 64.

30. See Rabbi Yoseph Caro, *Shulchan Aruch*. Orach Chayim, chapter 605.

The explanation is as follows: a pregnant woman becomes like two human beings[31]—her soul, her personality has become as two people. She now has two bodies, her own, with all its organs and vital arteries and the body she is carrying with all its own organs and life. Therefore, if she sinned while pregnant, it is as if two individuals sinned.

The same holds true with *ibbur*. The soul that is impregnated in the person becomes connected with his soul. It is now considered as if the person has two existences, and, therefore, the extra soul does not feel *extra*, and the person does not feel possessed by a strange soul.

There is, however, another form of impregnation, which is called a *dybbuk*, literally translated as 'attached.' It is commonly referred to as being possessed. This means that a person becomes possessed by another person's soul, or by an evil spirit. This dybbuk is a separate soul that never becomes unified with one's own soul, one's own distinct personality. Consequently, when a person is possessed by this other soul, he feels something external to his own existence now present, inhabiting and functioning within his body.

This notion of a man being possessed by external entities—souls or evil spirits—is an ancient belief found cross culturally, in many civilizations. It has been discovered that, in many early civilizations there were various rituals that the ancients believed would drive out these evil spirits. For example, singing, dancing, clapping of hands, or burning different incenses and so on.

In the Torah, this concept is referred to as a *Ruach Ra'ah*, an evil spirit. We find this mentioned in regard to the first

---

31. Rabbi M. M. Schneerson. *Likutei Sichot* (New York: Kehot Publication Society, 1983), Vol. 22, p. 59.

king of Israel, King Saul, when Saul was suffering from tremendous depression. The Torah states, "and the servants of Saul said to him: behold a spirit of the Lord which is evil is troubling you."[32] In the Talmud, this is also termed an evil spirit, and there is a discussion that reads as follows:[33] if a person travels farther than the set boundaries on *Shabbos* (according to the law of the Torah, a person may not leave beyond the limits of the city in which he resides) while possessed by an evil spirit, it was not he who exited the city's boundaries, it was the evil spirit within him that compelled him to do this action. If afterward, he comes back to his normal state of mind and wishes to re-enter the city, can he now be permitted to enter?[34]

In earlier times, this phenomenon of impregnation of an evil spirit was called a *Ruach Ra'ah*, which can either mean a demon or the spirit of the dead. However, from about the eighteenth century onward, this phenomenon became termed a dybbuk.[35] The word dybbuk means to become connected, thus connoting that another spirit connects itself with the person's soul, with his existence.

This concept of dybbuk was made popular by a Yiddish play written by S. Anski (a.k.a. Solomon Rapoport). The play was titled *The Dybbuk*.[36] It later on became a Yiddish and then

---

32. *Samuel 1*, chapter 16, verse 15.
33. Talmud. *Eruvin* 41b.
34. See *Ibid*. Rashi Titled. Ruach Ra. Rashi interprets this evil spirit to be a demon.
35. In numerous books from the greats of Israel from the eighteenth century onward. See, for instance, *Safer Habrit*. By Rabbi Pinchas Eliyahu Ben Meir of Vilna (1743–1821). (Jerusalem: Yerid HaSefarim, 1990), part 1, Maamor 17, chapter 15.
36. S. Anski, *The Dybbuk* (New York: Schoken Books, 1992).

a Hebrew play and then a movie, and, lately, it was adapted as a play on Broadway.

The gist of the story is as follows. Once upon a time, there lived two friends. When their wives became pregnant, they made a *truce*, that if one had a boy and the other a girl, the children would eventually marry. A short while after their agreement, one of the friends left town with his wife for a business deal. While on the way, the husband was killed, and his wife settled in another town and give birth to a boy, while the other wife gave birth to a beautiful little girl. And the vow was forgotten. Many years passed, and the boy, now an adolescent, came to that same town to study in the yeshiva and, incidentally, stayed as a guest in the home of his pre-destined bride (though he did not know it). As time progressed, they fell in love; however, her father would not even hear of such a match, for he wanted her to marry someone with money and prestige. Her father found her what he thought to be a suitable match, but she would not succumb, for she truly loved him, and he truly loved her. Her beloved realized, however, that he would never be able to marry her in this lifetime. The story goes on to tell us that from great pain and anguish he passed away. Before being led to her wedding, to her unwanted groom, she visited the gravesite of her beloved, to invite him from the worlds above to come down to the wedding. The story goes that as she is wailing at his gravesite, the spirit of her beloved enters her body as a dybbuk. She starts acting like him and speaking like him. The rabbis attempted all forms of exorcism, but to no avail. In the end, she actually died infatuated with the soul of her beloved.

In talmudic lore, *Ruach Ra'ah* refers only to souls being possessed by evil spirits or demons; however, in Kabbalah, we do find this idea of dybbuk, namely, a soul that possesses another person.

Rabbi Hayim Vital writes this is also used as a form of punishment for a wicked person.[37] After his demise, his soul will descend into the body of another wicked person and continuously feed the person information (e.g., terrible predictions about his future) to get him to do wicked deeds and basically control and confuse him (as in the discussion of the Talmud where the spirit makes him leave the boundaries on *Shabbos*).

The modern thinker, when confronted by such a fantastic tale, is immediately inclined to dismiss it as a psychological, neurological, or emotional disorder. In the following pages I will give voice to the skeptics refutations. (1) When a person is so infatuated or obsessed with another, that he takes on that person's personality and mannerisms. For example, in the play *The Dybbuk*, one can argue that it was not a dybbuk of her lover's soul that descended from above and inhabited her body, rather, it was she herself who was *acting* like her lover. She was so much in love with him that she couldn't fathom the idea of being married to someone else. She was so infatuated with his being, his personality, that she began acting and speaking like him. Thus, it was never an actual dybbuk of another spirit that entered her body; it was only she who was so attached to his personality that she traded her own personality for his and, accordingly, started acting like him.

(2) Or one can argue and say that in many environments, it is not possible for people to express how they really feel

---

37. *Safer Shar HaGilgulim*, Hakdamah 22. See also *Safer HaGilgulim*. Sader HaGilgulim. Ma'ase Noiraim, where it is stated that when another soul enters a body, it can cause harm spiritually.

Different Forms of Reincarnation: *Ibbur* and Dybbuk 119

about various issues, because of pressure from people around them and so on. For example, in a religious community (e.g., in the *shtetl*), especially in earlier times if people wanted to deviate from the prescribed way of living, it would be unthinkable to openly declare their intentions and urges, for they would then be immediately expelled and ostracized from their communities. Therefore, they attributed their desires to external entities. Not that they consciously made a decision to behave this way, rather, subconsciously they knew that the only way to express their feelings would be by attributing it to another entity. On a personal level, when there is something that is uncomfortable to say, we tend to say, "*they* say." Who is that "them" if not the person himself or herself? Thus, when a person comes along and claims a dybbuk is forcing him to sin, the truth might be that it is he who wishes to sin and the claimed dybbuk is just a cover up.

In male-dominant societies, whence women were not given the opportunity to express their opinions and feelings, it was quite common for women to act as if they were possessed by spirits and, in this way, express their true emotions. This can be found in Russian literature; for example, in Dostoyevsky's *The Brothers Karamazav*[38] and in Tolstoy's *The Kreutzer Sonata*,[39] they speak of women married to controlling men in a chauvinistic society who suffered from possession by evil spirits. This was their outlet for expression of their true feelings, without going against their societies. (Not that they consciously decided to act as if they were possessed by spirits; however, their subconscious compelled them to act this way, so that it could express itself. They are

---

38. See, *The Brothers Karamazav* (New York: Bantam Books, 1995), book 2, chapter 3.

39. See, *The Kreutzer Sonata* (New York: Signet Classic), p. 184.

so out of touch with who they really are that they themselves believe that it is not they who are expressing these forbidden feelings, but an external spirit.)

(3) Sometimes people possess certain weird and inappropriate desires. They may experience sordid and abnormal attractions, and, being that they are ashamed of these feelings, and cannot admit these feelings to other people (or even to themselves), they transfer the blame by believing that they are being possessed by devils, demons, or evil spirits. In Dostoyevsky's *The Possessed*, the protagonist, Mr. Stavrogin, is, throughout the novel, being possessed by demons and horrifying visions, until he is driven to kill himself. This was all caused by his forbidden love for a girl named Matryosha, which he cannot admit even to himself.[40]

Therefore, in these scenarios, the person suffering from these uncomfortable feelings subconsciously attributes these feelings to something external to himself, a *Ruach Ra'ah*, a demon, or a dybbuk. In psychology, we would term him to be a person who is afraid of himself, afraid of his true inner deep feelings, and, thus, he disclaims them and transfers them to an external spirit.

(4) It is also conceivable that the dybbuk is actually one's subconscious that is now speaking; it is like a dreamer's state of mind. A dream is "the royal road to the subconscious." A person can express in a dream certain feelings that, in a waking state, he wouldn't even dare think about. Moreover, in a dream, one can imagine that he is viewing someone else's temptation, and never has to accept that these temptations are actually his own. The same can be said

---

40. See, *The Possessed* (New York: Penguin Books, 1954), chapter 9 (Stavrogin confession).

with a dybbuk. The dybbuk's voice expressing itself is actually the person's inner quintessence, his subconscious.

(5) Historically and in literature,[41] we find this in reverse as well. If a person within a closed society wishes to deviate from the accepted path and actually commits a wrongdoing, the people around him, having difficulty accepting his actions, will attribute these declarations to outside influences, for example, demons or an evil spirit.

It is also quite common for people suffering from psychological disorders to imagine themselves possessed; however, their cure must come through a psychiatrist rather than a master of kabbalah.

A story is told about the great Talmudist Rabbi Chayim of Brisk (1853–1918). A woman once entered Reb Chayim's study, in a highly disturbed state, complaining that she was possessed by evil spirits and asking him to exorcise these evil spirits immediately. In those days, the alarm clock was a fairly new invention, and not many knew of its existence. Reb Chayim, on the other hand, was fortunate enough (being the rabbi of the city) to own one of these new gadgets. He took the alarm clock and set it to go off at midnight. Reb Chayim handed her the clock, telling her that if she heard a loud noise from this "special clock" after she fell asleep that night, this is a sign that the evil spirits are leaving her body. And so it was.

---

41. See, for instance, *The Nun* (New York: Viking Press, 1977), a satire by the French philosopher, Denis Diderot, where he writes that the nuns thought the girl was possessed, because she would not take a religious vow. See *The Scarlet Letter* (New York: Library of America, 1983), by the American writer, Nathaniel Hawthorne, where he writes in Chapter 6, "The Interview," that the jailer thought she—she, who committed the sin—was being possessed by Satan, because he felt she was not experiencing enough regret for her sin. See also *The Jewbird*, by Bernard Malamud in *The Stories of Bernard Malamud* (A Plume Book, 1983), where he writes about a dybbuk.

When the clock struck midnight and the alarm went off, she was instantly cured.[42]

One can also interpret the talmudic argument mentioned above to mean that the person who left the set boundaries of Shabbat was taken over by a *Ruach Ra'ah*, meaning that he temporarily went insane,[43] not that an actual external entity was in his body. It was his own insanity that caused him to deviate.

From the previous paragraphs, it is understood how difficult it is to discern if a person is actually possessed by an external entity. In fact, in order to be completely certain that this *Ruach Ra'ah* is an evil spirit and not just the person acting out his subconscious, or the like, the examiner must be a *Tzadik*, a true holy man.

Some sources maintain[44] that there are indeed a few visible differences between an true authentic dybbuk and a psychological disorder. One way is to observe from where the voice of the dybbuk emanates. If the source of the voice is from the mouth of the possessed, then we know it is not a real dybbuk; however, if the voice emanates from other areas of the possessed body, then we can confirm its authenticity. Another sign of a true dybbuk is a growth anywhere

---

42. Rabbi Pinchas Eliyahu Ben Meir of Vilna writes that most recorded cases of dybbuks are in fact mental instabilities which need to be cured by a physician. *Safer Habrit* part 1, Maamor 17, chapter 15.

43. See Talmud *Eruvin* 41b, the New Steinsaltz Edition. See also *Samuel 1*, chapter 15, verse 23, the commentary by Rabbi Dan Yitzchak Abarbanel, where he writes that *Ruach Ra'ah* (of King Saul) was the sickness of melancholia, where the person suffering this illness becomes frightened, and trembles with feelings of hopelessness.

44. The master kabbalist, Rabbi Moshe Zaccuto (1625–1697), *Igerret H'Ramaz*, question 2.

on the person's body.[45] Nonetheless, the true evaluation shall be done only through a *Tzadik*, a master of kabbalistic knowledge.

Whether or not one believes in the idea of dybbuk, it all comes down to one's belief in the great sages of Israel, the Gedolei Yisroel, who write about these concepts with certainty.

I once heard quoted in the name of the Lubavitcher Rebbe, "There is no evidence that they do *not* exist, and therefore it is more scientific to believe reliable witnesses." What this means is that, scientifically, we can never bring one hundred percent proof that a dybbuk does *not* exist. Therefore, says the rebbe, it is more scientific, i.e., it is more intellectually honest, to accept the testimony of the Gedolei Yisroel that dybbuk does exist.

---

45. Or, as others assert, the way to know if it is a real dybbuk rather than just a mental disorder, is to see if the person possessed is experiencing clairvoyance or predicting the future. If that is the case then it is a dybbuk; if not, let the possessed visit a psychiatrist. Rabbi Pinchas Eliyahu Ben Meir of Vilna, *Safer Habrit* part 1, Maamor 17, chapter 15.

6
Can We Remember Our Previous Incarnations?

There are many theologians, Jew and non-Jew alike, who argue the case for reincarnation based on the fact that there are many people who claim to remember their previous lives.[1] They profess memory of who and what they were in their previous lives. Furthermore, not only do they remember who they were, but they also recall when, where, and in which time they lived.[2]

There are those who argue that, from the very fact that there are people who remember their previous lives, we can establish as a concrete fact the concept of reincarnation. They say that this is proof that reincarnations do occur and one does not have to believe in this concept through faith. It can

---

1. Ian Stevenson, *Twenty Cases Suggestive of Reincarnation* (New York: American Society for Psychical Research, 1966); Geoffrey Hodson, *Reincarnation: Fact or Fallacy* (Wheaton, IL: The Theosophical Publishing House, 1967).

2. Ian Stevenson, *Twenty Cases Suggestive of Reincarnation* (New York: American Society for Psychical Research, 1966), p. 33.

be proven by human logic. (Rabbi Yakov Emdin states in regard to *Tzimtzumim* [constriction and concealment][3] that, even if this concept was not taught in Kabbalah, we would have realized it through our own intellect, for it is a logical conclusion of thought.) With the same sort of logic, many argue that the concept of reincarnation can be proven. Even if it hadn't been clearly stated in the Kabbalah, we would believe in these concepts on the basis of our own logical conclusions.

If the above is true and there are those who can remember their previous lives, why does it not apply to everyone? Why is it that there are those who do not remember their previous lives?[4]

There are those who attempt to answer this by saying that it is just like forgetting things that we have experienced in our existing lifetime (we forget at times what we ate for breakfast that same day). The further we are from our youth, the more we tend to forget those carefree days. The same holds true with remembering our previous incarnations. The further removed we are from our previous lives, the more we forget. Therefore, we find that there are children who do remember their previous lives; however, they begin to forget.[5] However, this explanation does not suffice, for, if this was the reason, we would all have some shred of memory of our previous lives, and this is not so.

---

3. Rabbi Yakov Emdin, *Matpachat Sefarim* (Jerusalem: Orech Tzadikim, 1995), chapter 9:64.

4. Dr. Brian Weiss, author of *Many Lives Many Masters* (New York: Simon and Schuster, 1988), in an interview in *Omni*, April 1994, p. 26.

5. Ian Stevenson, *Twenty Cases Suggestive of Reincarnation* (New York: American Society for Psychical Research, 1966), p. 113.

There are a few theologians who explain that the reason most people do not remember their previous lives is because, as the ancient Greeks explained in their mythology, after a person's demise, the first experience the soul has is the passage through the "River of Lethe."[6] This passageway was believed to cause the soul to forget all it experienced during its stay on this inferior plane. Therefore, they maintain, that when the soul reincarnates into this lowly world, it has no memory of its previous existence.

Interestingly, this notion of the "River of Lethe" appears to be quite similar to the concept of a "River of Fire," which the prophets speak about[7] and which the Talmud invokes as a punishment for the wicked.[8] Furthermore, in the Kabbalah[9] and Chassidus,[10] it is explained that this "River of Fire" is experienced by even the greatest of *Tzadikim*, whom, following their demise, must pass through this "River of Fire" before they can enter the lofty worlds of *Gan Eden*. Even angels must endure this process. For example, if an angel had descended into this physical world to execute a certain mission, then, prior to its ascent, it must also pass this "River of Fire."

When one desires the comprehension of a higher level of thought, he must first forget (to a certain extent) his lower

---

6. See Virgil (70–19 b.c.e.), *The Aeneid*.
7. *Daniel*, chapter 7, verse 10.
8. Talmud. *Chagigah*. 13b.
9. *Safer HaGilgulim*. Sader Gilgulim, chapter 11.
10. See Rabbi Schneur Zalman of Liadi. *Likutei Torah* (New York: Kehot Publication Society, 1996). Derushim LeShemini Atzeret, p. 84d. See also Rabbi Shalom Dovber, the fifth Chabad Rebbe, *Safer HaMaamorim—5679*. (New York: Kehot Publication Society, 1988), p. 281. (Rabbi Yehudah Loew, *Nesivot Olam* [Israel: 1990], Nosiv HaTorah, chapter 13.)

parameters of thought.¹¹ As expounded in Talmudic Lore,¹² a sage once traveled from Babylon to the Holy Land. In preparation for this move, he fasted 100 days. This was so that he should be able to forget all his previous learnings from Babylon, for he knew that the learning and understanding of the sages of Israel were on a much higher and deeper level than that of the sages of Babylon. Accordingly, Kabbalah explains that when a person dies and wishes to enter *Gan Eden*, his soul must first "shake off" all its previous prejudices, its physical experiences. The soul must immerse itself in the "Rivers of Fire" to force it to forget all its previous experiences.

The word for immersion in Hebrew is *Tovel* (טובל), which has the same four letters as the word for nullification in Hebrew, *Bittul* (בטול).¹³ When a person immerses himself in another entity (the waters of a *Mikvah*), his entire existence becomes encompassed and overwhelmed by its contents. Thus, when the soul immerses itself in this "River of Fire," it becomes nullified and loses its entire previous existence. Only then, after the soul became null and void, can it ascend into higher spiritual levels. This may perhaps be the reason why one forgets previous lives; however, it does not clearly state this in the Kabbalah.

There are theologians who believe[14] that, through the proper hypnosis, a person can recall his previous existences. Some say this can also be accomplished through appropriate

---

11. Rabbi Shalom Dovber, the fifth Chabad Rebbe, *Safer HaMaamorim—5672* (New York: Kehot Publication Society, 1977), pp. 1–50.

12. Talmud, *Bava Metzia* 85a.

13. Rabbi Schneur Zalman, *Siddur Eim Dach* (New York: Kehot Publication Society, 1965) "Intentions for the Mikvah" toward the end, p. 159.

14. Geoffrey Hodson. *Reincarnation: Fact Or Fallacy* chapter 6.

kabbalistic meditations. One of the simplest forms of meditation is what is termed internally directed, namely, asking oneself seriously, Who am I? What is my purpose? What do I want from life? And so on. One must ask these simple, yet monumental, questions without any interference. Nothing else should enter one's mind; one must be totally focused on his thoughts.

Through these simple meditations, one can become completely relaxed, in a quiet state of mind, and thus reach a higher state of consciousness. There are those who say that when one attains these levels (these higher states of consciousness) one can remember his previous lives.

There are also those who say that it is conceivable for a person to remember his previous life, when he is asleep and dreaming,[15] and thus in a higher state of consciousness.

There is a difference in a person's memories of his previous incarnations while asleep and while awake.[16] When one recalls one's previous existence in a waking state, it is as if he is viewing someone else's life being shown to him—one is as a spectator watching another's life displayed. However, when one remembers one's previous life during sleep, it is as if he is watching his own self in a different environment, in a different time and place. Yet, it is still the "you" that the story is showing. Therefore, it is quite common for someone to believe that which he dreamed even after waking. For example, a man dreams that he grew a beard, and upon waking, he runs to the mirror to see if there really is a beard on his face.

---

15. Dr. Weiss, an interview in *Omni*, April 1994.
16. Ian Stevenson. *Twenty Cases Suggestive of Reincarnation* (New York: American Society for Psychical Research, 1996), p. 321.

The above explanations assume that one should remember one's previous incarnations and thus, attempt to elucidate the reasons why one does not remember one's previous lives. However, according to Rabbi Chayim Vital's theory of reincarnation, the question of why we don't remember does not even come into play.

To understand the above statement, we must first understand the difference between the Eastern philosophies (which influenced the Western thinking) and the kabbalistic philosophy, as they apply to reincarnation.

According to Eastern thought, there is a "Wheel of Rebirth." This means that all souls must ultimately reach the level of "Nirvana"—a state in which it is completely detached from the mundane pleasures of the world, enlightened.[17] In Sanskrit, Nirvana means to "blow out," namely, to extinguish the fire of desire, hostility, and delusion.

Until the soul reaches this state, it is still attached to the physical world, and even death does not sever this connection. Therefore, after one's demise, the soul will, on its own, return to the physical world—reincarnate, time and again until it reaches "Nirvana." Hence, according to this way of thinking, the soul that reincarnates is the same exact soul each time and thus, is one continuous Karma.

However, according to the Kabbalah, the parts of the soul that reincarnate are not those that the previous person elevated. They are not the components of the soul which formed the personality and uniqueness of the previous person, rather, they are those areas of the soul with which the previous person had no contact or association.

Consequently, according to Eastern philosophy, it makes perfect sense to remember one's previous life, because the

---

17. See *Ibid*, p. 116.

previous person had the exact same soul as the present person. The Kabbalah's viewpoint, however, renders this highly improbable, for the parts of the soul that lived previously were of a completely different nature and personality than those which presently inhabit the person's body.

Many dismiss those who claim memory of a previous life as mentally or emotionally unstable and perhaps suffering from a split personality disorder because according to the Kabbalah, it seems unlikely that one would remember a previous life. However, some people do know certain facts about a previous existence that they would have no other way of knowing unless they had actually lived in that previous life. We are compelled to say that it is possible for people to remember aspects of their previous lives. How do we reconcile this with Kabbalah's way of thought?

There are ways through which one can indeed remember a previous incarnation that do not contradict the Kabbalah's philosophy.

One way is through the power of the supernatural. One must have the gift of *Ruach HaKodesh*. The Holy Spirit must rest upon a person in order for him to remember. One must be a great *Tzadik* with an exalted soul. There were various Tzadikim throughout the ages who would tell people what and where they were in their previous lifteimes.[18] The sainted Chassidic Rebbe, the Yismach Moshe (Rabbi Moshe Teitelbaum), once said of himself that he was one of the sheep of Yakov in a previous lifetime and one of the clansmen of Korach in another.[19]

---

18. *Safer Shar HaGilgulim*, toward the end.
19. See Jiri Langer, *Nine Gates to the Chassidic Mysteries* (New York: Behrman Inc. 1976), p. 167.

Even if one is not a *Tzadik*, through the proper discipline, it is possible for him to reach a higher state of consciousness and ultimately[20] (although highly unlikely), reach a level that enables one to experience a minor form of prophecy and, thus, behold the future as well as the past. Although, many Jewish philosophers[21] believe that prophecy can only be attained in a holy place (for example in the Holy Land of Israel),[22] they all agree that a lower level of divine revelation is possible elsewhere. When one reaches this level of prophecy, one does not actually experience memory of their previous incarnations, rather, a vision of those lifetimes, a glimpse into the past.

Another way to achieve memory of previous incarnations is by means of meditation. The previous people who contained this soul already elevated their particular part of the soul and that 'piece' of soul departed from the 'nucleus' of the soul. However, the soul of the present person did reside within the previous incarnations. Even though they had no obvious connection to it, it was somewhere deep in their subconscious. Therefore, through intense meditation and thus becoming in touch with one's subconscious, one can remember his previous lives. However, this is very difficult, and

---

20. There are a number of levels in divine revelations. The lower levels can be felt even outside the holy land. See Rabbi Yakov of Marve'ge, *Responsa from heaven* (Jerusalem: Mossad Harav Kook, 1957), in the introduction by Rabbi Reuven Margaliut. For many sources on this issues. See also Rabbi Pinchas Eliyahu Ben Meir of Vilna, *Safer Habrit*, part 2, Maamor 9, chapter 3.

21. Rabbi Saadiah Gaon, *Emunot VeDeyot*, Maamor 3, chapter 5. Rabbi Yehudah HaLevi, *The Kuzari*, Maamor 2, chapter 14. Rabbi Moshe Ben Nachman. *Ramban. Deuteronomy* Parshat Shoftim, chapter 18, verse 15. Rabbi Shelomo Ben Aderess. *Theshuvaht HaRahsba*, Teshuvah 548.

22. Midrash. *Mechilta on Shemot* Parsha 12, chapter 1. *Tanchuma* Parshat Bo, chapter 5. *Sifri on Devarim* 18:15.

there are not many who can achieve this. However, since one's (distinct) soul did indeed exist in a previous reincarnation, the 'you' of the soul was somewhere in the previous person's subconscious. As a result, at times one may experience *déjà vu*, whereupon, one feels that the experience he is going through occurred already in the past. Or, it may be that when one visits a distant land for the first time, one feels as though he had been there already. The reason the streets seem familiar is that, in a sense, he was already there.

There are other ways as well, through which a person can remember his previous existences. As explained in the previous chapter, impregnation (*ibbur*) can occur from within one's own soul. The parts of his general soul, which have already been elevated, descend into his present soul, to assist him with his elevations. In these instances, when his previous existence descends into his body, it may then be possible for him to remember his previous life, because the actual personality of his soul's previous life is now contained within his body.

Another form of *ibbur*, when one is impregnated with the soul of a departed *Tzadik*, can result in "memory" of a past life. However, in this case, when the person claims to remember his previous existence, he is actually remembering the life of the impregnated soul, the life of this *Tzadik*. And this can also occur in a negative sense. There can be a dybbuk, in which the soul of an evil person enters another person and tells him strange and foreign ideas, and the person may feel that these are memories of his own previous lives.[23]

I will now recount two well-documented and -publicized stories in which people believed they were remembering their

---

23. *Safer Shar HaGilgulim*, Hakdamah 30.

previous incarnations, when in truth they were being possessed by a departed soul, either in the form of an *ibbur* or a dybbuk.

The first case that we will analyze was recorded by Dr. Ian Stevenson,[24] titled "The Case of Jasbir." In the case study, there lived a child, Jasbir, whom at the age of 3 became severely ill, so ill in fact that at the peak of his illness, his parents actually thought that he died. However, he was revived and eventually recovered completely. When he started communicating again, he told a strange tale. He claimed to be another person and not Jasbir. He told his parents of a different family to whom he belonged, living in a different city many miles away. His family went to investigate his story and see if what he was claiming was true. They came to the city of which the boy spoke, and they found indeed that there was such a person living in this city who died at same exact time that the little boy Jasbir was sick. The parents then concluded that their son must now be a reincarnation of the deceased man.

At first glance, this seems to be a clear case of reincarnation. However, upon further examination it appears that what occurred was not *gilgul* (reincarnation), because reincarnation begins at time of birth, whereas Jasbir and the deceased man were both alive in this world at the same time. Thus, we understand that rather than reincarnation, Jasbir was actually experiencing an *ibbur* or a dybbuk from the other person's soul.

In the Kabbalah,[25] it tells of a certain reincarnation that occurs when one is life-threateningly ill. (It can also occur when

---

24. Ian Stevenson, *Twenty Cases of Suggestive Reincarnation* (New York: Kehot Publication Society, 1966), p. 33.
25. *Safer Shar HaGilgulim*, Hakdamah 5. See also *Benei Aharon*, Hakdamah 5.

one becomes extremely angry.²⁶) One's soul may ascend from his body, and a new soul descends to take its place, thereupon rejuvenating the sick body and giving it new life. At first glance, it seems that this is what occurred with Jasbir; however, looking into it a little further, we realize that this was not the case with Jasbir for if the soul of the deceased man had replaced Jasbir's soul, the soul that would have come into Jasbir would have had a different "you" than the deceased man. Therefore, although perhaps Jasbir would have acted differently being that he was now possessed of a new soul, he would not have had the memories of the deceased man. Therefore, we conclude that it must have been an *ibbur* or a dybbuk.

The second case that we will analyze is documented by Dr. Brian Weiss.²⁷ The study is titled, "The Case of Catherine." It reads as follows: there was a woman named Catherine who through hypnosis would relay messages to Dr. Weiss that she received from the "Master's souls." In this case, because she is transmitting a message from someone else, it is understood that it is not *her* soul, her *gilgul*, that is revealing these messages, rather it is a form of *ibbur* or dybbuk that is the revealer. She also recalled her "previous lives"; however, we understand that they are not actually her own previous lives, rather the lives of the *ibbur* or dybbuk that reside within her.

This point holds true in regard to another documented case study, in which Dr. Weiss records a case of a woman who not only remembered her past life, but in addition was able to predict the future with stunning accuracy. It is quite

---

26. Ibid. See also Rabbi Chayim Yoseph David Azulay, *Morah Be'etzba*. (Brooklyn: Ateret, 1987), chapter 1:10. Rabbi Levi Yitzchak of Bardichov (1740–1809), *Kedushat Levi*. Likutim p. 210.

27. Dr. Brian Weiss, *Many Lives Many Masters* (New York: Simon and Schuster, 1988).

clear that predicting the future has naught to do with remembering one's past through *gilgul*. Hence, we are compelled to say that this woman was experiencing an *ibbur* or dybbuk of a departed soul. Dybbuk, as mentioned earlier, tells the body exactly what is going on in the world, what has previously occurred, and what *will happen*, and thus like.

In conclusion, when one is in a natural state of being, it is very unlikely that one would possess memories of previous lives, and, hence, when we chance to meet those who do "remember," it may be possible that it is not through *gilgul* that they remember, rather through an *ibbur* or dybbuk.[28]

The soul—the "you" of the soul which reincarnates into a lower creature as a punishment, does remember its previous existence in the human form. In this case the "you" of the soul reincarnates into the lower creature, and the memory of what it was, comparative to its present state, is precisely its punishment, its refinement.[29]

---

28. Rabbi Menasha Ben Israel, *Nishmat Chayim*, Maamor 3, chapter 15. There is no memory of previous incarnations. See: Rabbi Moshe Corodovero *Shiur Komah* (Israel: 1966) chapter 4, p. 166. Rabbi Shirmon Ben Tzemah Duran *Magen Avot* (Livorno: 1785) part 3, p. 88A.

29. Rabbi Eliezer Ezcary, *Sefer Cheraidim*, chapter 33.

7
Can Reincarnation Be Proven?

There are four fundamental reasons why many believe in the concept of reincarnations.[1] Two of them are ideological and religious reasons, reasons that apply only if one believes in a Moral and Just God, "divine justice." And two are factual reasons, proofs from various phenomena that occur in this universe.

In reference to the religious and ideological, I must stress that there are two completely different paths in the belief of God. There is the "God of the philosophers"—God as the "uncaused cause"—or supreme Being. And there is the "God of Abraham, Isaac, and Jacob," a God who is intimately involved in His creations, Who cares or chooses to care about and empathize with His creations—a God of worship. The

---

1. Geoffrey Hodson, *Reincarnation: Fact or Fallacy* (Wheaton, Illinois: The Theosophical Publishing House, 1967), chapter 1.

difference between these beliefs is the difference between belief in God's existence and belief in God Himself.[2]

The ideological reasons to believe in reincarnation must be based on belief in God Himself, believing that God is involved in creation and is the Master of justice. Furthermore, one must also believe that the world at large, and the individual human being in particular, was created for a divine purpose. With the basis of these beliefs, these 'proofs' can be applied.

We observe the world around us and are shown so much suffering and pain, so often to those who seem to be the least deserving of punishment, the children and the righteous. This raises a much asked and deliberated question—Are these acts of a just God, is this true justice? Some use reincarnation as a measure of comfort and explanation in this troubling question. They conclude that, since it is possible for one to suffer a "punishment"—a refinement—for a wrongdoing committed in a previous lifetime,[3] we can justify the suffering of the innocent[4] by saying that the reason they are being punished is for the sins they committed in their previous incarnations.[5] In other words, because we believe that God is just, there must be reincarnation.

---

2. See Rabbi Yehudah HaLevi, *The Kuzari*. Maamor 4, chapter 16.

3. Talmud, *Shabbat* 119b.

4. See *Safer HaBahir*, Number 195. Rabbi Yitzchak of Acco, *Meirat Einayim*, Parshat Bereishit 4:1. Rabbi Mayor Eben Aldavia, *Shivilei Emunah*, Nosiv Thishihei (Jerusalem: 1990), p. 374. Rabbi Moshe Alshich, *Deuteronomy* chapter 7, verse 9, 10. Rabbi Meir Ben Gabbai, *Avodat Hakodesh*, part 2, chapter 32. Rabbi Yeshayah Halevi Horowitz, *Shallah HoKodesh*, Shnei Luchot Habrit Safer Bamidbar Devarim, Ki Tetze. Rabbi Naphtali Hirtz Bacharach, *Emek HaMelech*, Hakdamah 2, chapter 3. Rabbi Menasha Ben Israel, *Nishmat Chayim*, Maamor 4, chapter 11. Rabbi Moshe Chayim Luzzatto, *Derech Hashem*, part 2, chapter 3. Rabbi Shem Tov Ben Shem Tov Safer Ha'emunot (Jerusalem: 1969), Shar 7, chapter 4.

5. See *Ramban*, Rabbi Moshe Ben Nachman, *Job*, chapter 33. Where he writes, that the punishments to Job—who was a *Tzadik*—were for sins com-

(It should be noted that, according to the Eastern way of thought, the question is not, why God places souls in "unjust" situations; rather, why does the soul itself choose to descend into suffering? They believe that the soul itself actually has the *choice* which body to inhabit. Therefore, it happens that the soul will choose to inhabit a "vessel of suffering," in order for the soul to gain a greater experience, to learn more, and thus become even more "Enlightened."[6])

Another proof for reincarnation from an ideological point of view is by obtained through close examination of the life and destiny of a human being. What is man's ultimate destiny? Man is replete with selfish temptations, he lives his life in spiritual darkness encountering disease, depression, and conceit. It is not conceivable that man should live his life with spiritual restraints and suffering and then die without ever ridding himself of his evil inclinations and freeing himself from the spiritual void around him. It seems impossible that spiritually, a man could live in vain. And to resolve this anomaly, one may offer the conclusion that although a human being may not attain the status of a spiritually "perfect man in a single lifetime," nevertheless, through numerous reincarnations, the soul can ultimately attain this level of perfection. Each time the soul descends upon this earth, it can attain at least one level of perfection, and thus what one fails to achieve in one's present lifetime, one can rectify in the next reincarnation. In summary, from a purely ideological stand-

---

mitted in a previous *gilgul*, and the same holds true, he writes, with any *Tzadik* who suffers. See, *Zohar*, Parshat Ki Tetze; *Safer Shar Hagilgulim*, Hakdamah 15.

6. Dr. Brian Weiss, in an interview in *Omni*, April 1994, p. 26. See also Rabbi Avraham Azulay, *Chesed LeAvraham*, part 4, chapter 11. Where he seems to suggest that, essentially, according to Kabbalah, it is also the soul that ultimately chooses.

point, because man must have a destiny and purpose for living, there must be reincarnation.

There are those who consider reincarnation to be a purely logical conclusion, based on empirical knowledge.

There are children who seem to have been born with unusually advanced and developed talents. They are usually labeled "child prodigies." There are those who maintain that the natural talents people are born with are inherited talent from their previous lifetimes. What usually takes many years of extensive diligent study can be reached very easily by these child prodigies because they inherited these talents from their previous incarnations, and the person in the incarnation preceding theirs already underwent the struggle necessary to achieve this great level of skill.

There are also people who claim to remember with supreme accuracy their previous existence. And to some this may seem as conclusive evidence of reincarnation. However, as previously explained, what may seem to some as memory, is usually caused by other factors and there is rarely, if ever, memory that transfers from incarnation to the next.

The above "proofs" for reincarnation were offered by those who view reincarnation from a perspective other than the Torah.

I will now proceed to compare these "proofs" with the views of the Torah.

The first theological proof mentioned above is based on the belief in a Just and Moral God.

Belief in a Just God is a fundamental tenet in the Torah. As King David states in Psalms, "A righteous God You are, in all Your ways."[7] Thus, the question is, can reincarnation

---

7. *Psalms*, chapter 145, verse 17.

from a Torah perspective explain away the suffering of the innocent?

The Torah states, "A person through his own sins shall perish."[8] This means that each human being is judged according to his own actions, for the sins that he himself committed, and *not* for those committed by other people, even when the people in question are his own ancestors. When a person is reincarnated, his present self is its own personality, a completely new creation. It is, therefore, highly unlikely that this new person would be punished for actions done in an earlier incarnation.

This is especially true when it comes to the suffering of children. When a newly born infant suffers, the punishment is not so much for the child as it is for the parents.[9] The parents are those who suffer the most, they are the ones who receive the brunt of the punishment. Therefore, although reincarnation may offer an explanation for the child's suffering, it is not all inclusive, it does not include the reason for the punishment the parents receive.

Hence, in general, punishments do not carry over from one incarnation to the next, because people are judged for their own actions and not for actions done by another. The

---

8. *Deuteronomy*, chapter 24, verse 16.
9. See Talmud. *Shabbat* 32b. Where the Talmud states, "For the sins . . . (this refers specifically to the sin of a broken vow) of parents, children are punished to die at a young age." This statement seems to suggest that children are punished for sins committed by their ancestors. Nonetheless, we can say that the death of their children is the parents' punishment, for they suffer most. And the reason why they—the innocent children—suffer is for other reasons as we will try to explain later on in this chapter, but not for their ancestors' sins, for each individual person is judged and responsible for his or her own actions.

reincarnated soul is a new being and not a continuum of its previous existence.[10]

(Although we find it stated in the Kabbalah,[11] that the Ten Sages of Israel were punished for the sin of the Ten Tribes who sold Joseph. They were punished for someone else's sins! This is explained in depth in Chapter 6. In short, it was not through reincarnation, but through *ibbur*.[12])

A question was posed to the Lubavitcher Rebbe, Rabbi Menachem M. Schneerson.[13] There was a little girl who had passed away, prior to the age of Bat Mitzvah, 12 years. Her parents wrote a letter to the Rebbe, asking for an explanation. They wanted to understand why her soul descended if she had never been obligated to do a mitzvah? (The obligation begins at 12 years for a girl.) What was the purpose of her soul's descent?

The Rebbe began his response by stating, first and foremost, that it is nearly impossible for any human being to be certain of God's ultimate intention.

In this present-day, all souls descend as a continuation of their incarnations—to complete what they had previously left unfinished.

It is sometimes possible that a soul leaves this earth at a tender age because its preceding incarnation had passed away before its allotted time, and those years had to be lived. However, this is not the norm, as most people are able to live out their predestined life-span.

---

10. See, however, the sources quoted in this chapter, footnote 4 and 5.
11. *Safer Shar HaGilgulim*, Hakdamah 36.
12. See Chapter 6. See also *Safer Sader Gilgulim*, chapters 5 and 16.
13. See *Torah't Menachem. Menachem Tzion* (New York: Kehot Publication, 1995), part 2, p. 568.

No person, no matter how Godly and what lofty levels he may have attained, can know with certainty the true intentions of God. And we conclude that, it may happen, albeit rarely, that a child will die at a young age as a continuation of his previous incarnation. However the punishments of the previous existences do not carry over into their bodies. They do not suffer for another's sins, rather, they reincarnate "to fulfill what they had missed previously."

It is recounted in the tales of the *Baal Shem Tov*, that he would console the parents of children who had died by telling them that the souls of these innocent children were lofty and elevated, and had only to descend into this lowly world for a short period of time, in order to *complete* the mission that they were originaly sent down to accomplish. Thus, because they were truly righteous people in their previous incarnations and were lacking only the slightest of elevations, they could complete their task in a very brief period of time.

Rabbi Saadiah Gaon was indeed correct in stating that we cannot bring proof for reincarnations from the fact that we witness the innocent suffering.[14] (He writes elsewhere in his book[15] that some people may suffer in this physical world in order to receive a greater reward in the world to come.)

The monumental question, which leads many to believe in reincarnation,[16] is; Why do the innocent suffer? Why do bad things happen to good people? This is one of the oldest and most complex of all theological questions ever posed. The nature of the human mind is such that it attempts to make

---

14. Rabbi Saddiah Gaon, *Emunot VeDeyot*, at the end of Maamor 6.
15. See *Ibid* (Jerusalem: Haamnim, 1993), Maamor 5.
16. Rabbi M. M. Schneerson, *Igrot Kodesh* (New York: Kehot Publication Society, 1989), vol. 13, p. 203.

sense of life, as we experience it; its joys as well as its sorows. When faced with tragedy, we endeavor to find its place in the puzzle of life. Yet it seems not to belong within this puzzle, and aberration in our reality. In our minds we perceive the world as an orderly sequence of events. One's actions will cause a reaction, and so on. A "senseless" tragedy leaves us bewildered and betrayed. Thousands of minds over thousands of years have felt this pain and asked this question. I have gathered the "classic interpretation" and in the following pages, will present them to you.

Moses asked of God,[17] "Show me Your ways?"[18] The Talmud teaches that what Moses was really asking of God was; "Show me Your inner ways, reveal to me Your inner intentions . . . why do the righteous suffer while the wicked prosper?"

Throughout centuries of Jewish thought, there were many philosophical as well as mystical reasons and interpretations for the tragedies and sorrows that occur to the good, righteous people.[19]

The noted mystic and moralist, Rabbi Moshe Chaim Luzzatto,[20] writes, God's purpose in creation was to bestow the greatest possible goodness upon His creations.[21] For His creations to fully appreciate the goodness they are receiving, they must deserve the good, for if the goodness bestowed upon humans by God is not a deserved reward, then it will lessen the recipient's pleasure, by the feelings of shame that always accompany undeserved rewards. (This is what the

---

17. See Talmud. *Berachot* 7a.
18. *Numbers*, chapter 33, verse 13.
19. See for example, Rabbi Saadiah Gaon, *Emunot VeDeyot*, Maamor 5; Rabbi Schneut Zalman of Liadi, *Tanya*, chapter 26.
20. See *Derech HaShem*, part 1, chapter 2.
21. See also: Rabbi Saadiah Goan, *Emunot VeDeyot*, end of Maamor 1.

Kabbalah terms *Nahama DiKisufa*, "shameful bread"—sustenance that is given without work.)[22] The reason then that God created evil in this world and the opportunity for man to do bad deeds, is so that His creations will have a struggle between good and evil and through the struggle they will choose the good over the evil and be deserving of God's abundant goodness.

Although this answer may explain evil that man himself perpetrates, it does not extend to those God causes unto man, such as famine and starvation.[23]

There is an interpretation based on a talmudic tale.[24] A pagan once asked of the saintly sage Rabbi Akiva the following question: If your God is truly a Lover of the poor, as you assert, then why does He not sustain them? Rabbi Akiva answered him, "In order to save man from *Gehenom*," namely, through observing suffering in our fellow humans on this earth, we will be moved to compassion and empathy. It is through caring and compassion that a person can be saved from *Gehenom*.

This answer appears to explain why God created suffering and evil in general.

The mystics offer the following interpretation.[25] Of the ten sefirot, the sefirah of *Gevurah* seems to us the most harsh.

---

22. Jerusalem Talmud, *Orlah*, chapter 1, Halacha 3. Talmud, *Kedushin*, 36b. *Tosefot*, Kall. Rabbi Yoseph Caro. *Magid Mesharim* (Jerusalem: Orah, 1960), Parshat Bereishit, p. 10. Rabbi Schneur Zalman of Liadi, *Likutei Torah* (New York: Kehot Publication Society, 1996). Parshat Tzav. Page 7d. Rabbi Moshe Chaim Luzzatto. *Da'at Tevunoth*, in the beginning. By the same author, *KaLaCh Pischei Chochmah* number 4.

23. See Rabbi Moshe Chaim Luzzatto, *Da'at Tevunoth*, where he touches upon this issue.

24. See Talmud. *Bava Batra* 10a.

25. See for example, Rabbi Schneur Zalman of Liadi, *Tanya*, chapter 26.

It is the antithesis of *Chesed*, which is the light of Godliness in a revealed and open form, appearing to us as acts of kindness, whereas *Gevurah* is representative of strength and power, the aptitude for concealment of all that is holy. Yet, the mystics teach that the *Sefirah* of *Gevurah* originates from a loftier source then that of *Chesed*.

There are, in general, two forms of God's benevolence. One is the *revealed kindness*, kindness that remains in a revealed way when it descends below. This Divine energy emanates from the *Sefira* of *Chesed*. However, there is a form of kindness that emanates from the *Sefira* of *Gevurah* (whose source, as explained, is even higher than that of *Chesed*). When this kindness appears in our physical, finite, and terrestrial sphere, we experience it as deeds of strength, or prevalence. Since its source is so exalted and lofty, when it finally reaches us, we feel it to be too much to absorb. This can be compared to a teacher and his student. If the student is, approximately, in the same intellectual domain as his teacher, then the student feels that he is receiving a kindness from the teacher when the teacher reveals a thought to him. The student understands that his teacher is sharing a thought with him. However, if the teacher is Einstein, and he attempts to teach the theory of relativity to a student of low intellectual capabilities, then not only does the student not feel grateful for the lesson, but on the contrary, he feels that the teacher is overwhelming him and is acting cruelly. The same holds true when God reveals His kindness to His creations. *Chesed* is a lower *Sefira*. It is a *Sefira* that is more connected with the world, and, therefore, when revealed to us, we feel it to be a kindness. However, the *Sefira* of *Gevurah* is so much higher than our own lowly world that when it is revealed to us we do not feel the goodness of the deed; on the contrary, we feel that we are being overwhelmed and that we are suffering. Thus, the Mystics conclude, we should be aware that when we experience an act of *Gevurah* from God, an act of strength, it is actually an extreme act of kindness, so lofty that in its descent, we feel it as a punishment.

All the above answers and, indeed, all the explanations *ever* offered are only interpretations that concern the world such as it is *after* God created it to function in this manner. For example, in this world, as we know it, the only way for a person to show his compassion is through others who are in *need* of his compassion. However, God in His infinite wisdom could have created the world with other truths, different realities. God could have created a world in which a human being can show compassion even when there is no one around to receive the compassion. God could have created a world in which a person could have freedom of choice, and yet the world would contain no evil!

Although the above appears to be contradictory, for without downtrodden there is no need for compassion, and without evil, good is obvious and there is no real choice, however, we are talking about the Omnipresent, an all-powerful Infinite Being, One who is above and beyond any human comprehension. Thus, it is understood that God can do what we think to be the impossible. Hence, God could have created the world in such a way that the highest forms of goodness would descend to the lowest levels of creation and still remain revealed acts of goodness and kindness. Thus, it is understood that all the above answers and any explanation that human comprehension may offer are not the true, ultimate answer.

And, therefore, the ultimate conclusion to all these questions is found in Job.[26, 27] "Why do the wicked live healthy, with an abundance of wealth?" Why do the wicked prosper while he, Job (one who was considered to be an extremely righteous person[28]) continues to suffer? Job does not accept the answer given to him by his friends, namely, that he is suffering because of the sins he had committed. Ultimately, at the end of the story, God answers Job and tells him, "I am God, I am the Creator of the universe, and you are but a tiny creature in this immense universe. Where were you when the universe was created?"[29] God is telling Job that, being that he is only a finite creature, he will never fully comprehend the ways of an infinite God. As the Master Prophet declares,[30] "for My thoughts are not your thoughts, and your ways are not My ways." At the end of the story, Job surrenders and says, "It is beyond my comprehension, and thus I do not know."[31] As the Mishnah states,[32] "It is not in our hands, we cannot understand, it not the prosperity of the wicked nor the suffering of the righteous."

The human mind functions in a space/time capsule. Our minds operate through the dimensions of time and space. We cannot even try to comprehend something that is above these parameters. As a rational being, we like to think that everything makes sense; that if we were to add one and one, it would

---

26. See Talmud. *Bava Batra* 15a, where it is stated that, according to one opinion, Job lived in the times of Yakov. This means to tell us, that the question was relevant from the times of antiquity.
27. *Job*, chapter 21, verse 7.
28. See *Job*, throughout, for example, the beginning of chapter 32.
29. *Ibid*, chapter 38, verse 4.
30. *Isaiah*, chapter 55, verse 8.
31. *Job*, chapter 42, verse 3.
32. *Avot*, chapter 4. Mishnah 15.

surely be two. When we are witness to one and one (one=doing good, plus one=being rewarded) equalling three (being punished), we are puzzled, and immediately try to make sense of the punishment by rationalizing that it is really one plus one. Either the person was not so righteous (because of sins he had done in a previous life) and he deserved the punishment, or the punishment is really not a punishment. However, the one true answer can only be that we do not know.

The true, absolute answer to all these questions is that God has His reasons, and ultimately it is He alone who understands (albeit, on a different level of thought) these ideas. One's comfort may come from one's trust in God that He is doing what is best for us.

This fact can be illustrated with a metaphor. A person with no previous knowledge of medicine must undergo a very serious operation to remove a sick organ in the body, and it must be done immediately. He will undergo the operation. He knows that the doctors around him understand the procedure, and he has trust in them. However, if a small child were to walk into the same operating room whilst the patient, his father, is being operated on, he would certainly assume that the doctors are cold-blooded killers, while in fact, they are saving his life.

The above metaphor concerns humans, possessed of human intelligence. One may be more advanced than the other, perhaps more knowledgable and mature, yet both their minds are within the same genre. How much greater the disparity between the mind of a human and the "mind" of God. If one is spiritually attuned, he will realize that what God bestows upon mankind stems only from His goodness. At times it is goodness that manifests itself as revealed goodness, and at times it is goodness that is experienced as a deed of strength. However, one who is spiritually alienated is like a child who perceives the doctors as murderers!

Although we accept as truth that God has His reasons for the suffering of mankind, it does not mean that we are forced to surrender to our suffering, and say, "This is the will of God, and so be it." On the contrary, we can believe so strongly in God that in times of distress we will say that although God may have His reasons, being that He is the Almighty Omnipresent God, He can give us even the greatest kindnesses in a revealed way. By entreating out to God, we are not demonstrating a lack of reverence and belief in Him, quite the opposite, we are showing that our belief in God has no boundaries!

We will now examine the other ideological proof that some offer as substantiation for reincarnation and the Torah's perspective regarding this. Man must ultimately elevate himself beyond his physical limitations and therefore one must reincarnate until this has been accomplished. Man has a destiny. Therefore, there must be reincarnation.

There is an essential difference in the way the Torah views life and the manner in which the rest of society (which is generally a Christian society) views the world. To a certain extent, the difference is even more pronounced when it comes to the way the societies of the East (the Hindus, Buddhists, Taoists, and so on) view life; the purpose of creation, and the purpose of the soul's descent.

According to the way the majority of the world views religion,[33] the ultimate idea of holiness and thus, supreme

---

33. See for example, Jacob Neusner, *A Rabbi Talks with Jesus* (New York: Image Books, Doubleday, 1993) which illustrates how the Christian view of life is to create a kingdom in heaven, while the Jews' is to create a kingdom on earth. See: Rabbi Eliyahu Ben Amozegh (1823–1900), *Be'Shevilei Mussar* (Israel: Mossad Harav Kook, 1966), for an halachic perspective on this issue.

expression of spirituality is soul. Anything besides our soul is a concealment of holiness. Thus, the human body is perceived accordingly, as a hindrance to the soul. The body is viewed in a negative fashion.[34] Consequently, if a person wishes to live a holy life, he must first totally detach himself from the physical reality, the body. He must live life as an ascetic. He must become a reclusive hermit, living in celibacy, and not succumbing to his natural instincts for marriage. The ultimate destiny is to create a kingdom for God in heaven and not on this earth.[35] According to these beliefs, faith is the most important ingredient for salvation. Therefore, they are left with an obvious dilemma. How can a life replete with animalistic temptations be the ultimate destiny for man? And thus, they conclude that there must be reincarnation of the soul.

However, according to the Torah, the purpose of creation and the Godly soul's descent to this lowly physical world is (refer to Chapter 3); "To create a dwelling place for God on this earth."[36] The soul descends in order to elevate the physical, to transform the material into a spiritual existence. As the Talmud explains,[37] after Moses received the Torah, the heavenly angels came to God, with a complaint, "Why has the Torah been given to lowly creatures such as humans? Are we not the spiritual creatures, the ones who can truly appreciate the holy Torah?" To this, Moses responded that the entire pur-

---

34. This idea is expressed in their theology throughout and is beautifully illustrated by the German writer Thomas Mann, in *The Magic Mountain* (New York: The Modern Library, 1992), chapter titled "Operations Spirituals."

35. See for instance, *Matthew* 10:34–37; 12:46–50.

36. See Midrash *Tanchuma*. Parshat Naso. Chapter 16. (See: *Tanya*. Chapter 36.)

37. See Talmud. *Shabbat* 88b. See Rabbi M. M. Schneerson, *Likutie Sichot* (New York: Kehot Publication Society, 1982), volume 18, page 28.

pose of the Torah is to elevate and transform the physical, to live in a physical world and serve God there, to do His *mitzvot* and achieve elevation, through working *with* one's corporeal existence and not through transcending it.

The objective of the Godly soul's descent upon this world is *not* for transcendance of its body's physical temptations and desires, to rise above his bodily temptations[38] and self.[39] On the contrary, the principal function of man's creation is that he should elevate his body; his physicality. God wishes for us[40] to continuously struggle and, thus, constantly overcome our evil/selfish instincts, transforming them into holiness. Man's destiny in life is *not* to metamorphose into a heavenly spirit such as an angel, without temptations for evil, but rather, to be a person of conflicts and overcome them, to coexist with the physical, whilst raising it to the spiritual. One must have a healthy, strong body with which to serve God.[41] As the holy Maggid of Miezricz (?–1773), Rabbi Dovber, once phrased it,[42] "A small hole in the body is a colossal cavity in the soul."

The purpose of the soul's descent is not for its own personal gain. The soul does not enter the body to obtain new and deeper spiritual experiences. Rather, the purpose is to

---

38. See Talmud. *Tannit* 11a, where the Talmud maintains that he who cannot fast because of health reasons and does so anyway is considered a sinner!

39. In the Talmud in numerous places (for example, *Tannit* 11a), it is stated that a *Nazir*—he who refrains himself from drinking wine and cutting his hair—is considered a sinner.

40. See *Tanya*, chapters 12, 13, 14, 27. And generally throughout the Tanya.

41. Rambam, *Hilchot De'ot*, chapter 4, Halacha. 1. Rabbi Schneur Zalman of Liadi. *Tanya* (New York: Kehot Publication Society, 1965). Chapters 12, 13, 14, 27.

42. See Rabbi Yisroel Baal Shem Tov, *Keter Shem Tov* (New York: Kehot Publication Society, 1974) in the HoSofot. See also *BeTziel HaChochmah* (Israel: Kollel Avrechem Chabad, 1987), p. 28.

elevate the body in which it resides. This is a goal which the soul can attain, even in the span of a single lifetime, through the fulfillment of God's will. The majority of people cannot transcend their *entire* physical reality in a single incarnation; however, as this is not their ultimate function, it does not negate a higher destiny. The overwhelming majority of people must strive to serve God, despite their evil/selfish inclinations. This is our destiny.

Thus the views of other religions, regarding the descent of the soul are the complete antithesis of those of the Torah. While the former view the soul's descent as being solely for its own aggrandizement, the Torah explains the soul's journey to this earth as a mission of elevation of the body, indeed, of all physicality. Yet, throughout its quest, the soul itself *does* become elevated. However, this was not the purpose for its descent, rather the reward for the same. Our sages tell us that[43] "God does not withhold the rightful reward from any living creature." This includes the soul, which although spiritual, is still a living creation and must therefore be rewarded for its struggles. The soul's reward is through the fulfillment of the 613 precepts, which are analogous to its 613 "segments." Through repeated incarnations the soul is eventually elevated in its entirety.

As previously mentioned, there are those who will substantiate reincarnation solely by observing an occurrence of nature such as the existence of children who have been discovered to be "prodigies." There are the child prodigies who are physically gifted, and there are those whose gifts lie in the realm of spiritually. A physically gifted child prodigy might show tremendous ability in music or fine arts, or countless other ares (as is documented in regard to the great musi-

---

43. See Talmud, *Bava Kamma* 38b, *Nazir* 23b.

cian Mozart, who composed music prior to the age of four). A spiritually gifted child prodigy will show exceptional spiritual powers that seem way beyond youthful spiritual capacities. These two phenomena are attributed, by some, to reincarnation. These people conclude that these gifted children inherited these abilities from their previous incarnation.

In the Kabbalah, it speaks often and openly regarding spiritual prodigies. The mystics termed this wonder a *Yinukah*.[44] A *Yinukah* contains a soul that was previously contained within a *Tzadik* who had elevated his entire soul. Since this soul is now entirely elevated, it need not reincarnate for the purpose of elevation. This soul now reincarnates into another human being, the aforementioned *Yinukah*, not for its own aggrandizement, rather to assist other lost and confused souls. Having established this, it makes perfect sense that this *Yinukah*, who contains within him the elevated soul, has the potential to reveal all the layers of his soul with little or no effort.[45]

This type of reincarnation differs from the more commonly experieneed one, for in the latter, the previous incarnation's distinct part of soul does not reincarnate again. The personality of the previous person goes on to receive its rewards in *Gan Eden* after its body's demise. The following incarnation is *not* a continuation of the previous one. In such a case, one would, understandably, not inherit the talents of his earlier existence.

However, in a case of *Yinukah*, the entire personality of the previous incarnation now reincarnates into this second

---

44. *Zohar*, Parshat Balak, Maamor Yinuka. See *Shar HaGilgulim*, Hakdamah 7.

45. See *Ibid.*, Rabbi Avraham Azulay, *Chesed LeAvraham*, part 5, chapter 21.

human being, and, therefore, whatever talents he had possessed will transfer to the *Yinukah* as well.⁴⁶

There have been documented cases in which it was concluded that the person in question was a reincarnation of a Torah sage who had lived before him. In 1955, there was a child in Israel who, at a very young age, knew the entire Talmud. He was then presumed by many leading Torah personalities of the time, to be a clear example of a *gilgul* of a Torah sage.⁴⁷

This proof of reincarnation, which is founded on the basis of child prodigies, will only hold true with *Yinukah*, which is a rare form of *gilgul*. With the majority of cases of *gilgul*, however, this will not suffice as substantial proof.

If one accepts the popular view of reincarnation as a continuous karma in which each incarnation inherits the personality of its previous life, then it would seem strange that we do not find a reincarnation of every great person who ever lived in each generation.

According to the Kabbalah, it is understood that even though there have been many great talents and geniuses over time, their reincarnations may not have reflected their greatness, for their reincarnations had no memories of their previous existence, being that they were in contact with an entirely different part of their soul.

---

46. Talmud. *Tannit* 9a, where the Talmud mentions a *Yinukka*, a child who showed great genius at a very young age. (However, we can say that the Talmud is only talking about this *Yinukka* showing signs of genius in Torah, which would then be in the category of a spiritual prodigy, and there would then be no proof—at least from the Talmud—regarding prodigies in general! Nevertheless, see *Shar HaGilgulim*, Hakdamah 38, for a stronger indication about child prodigies in general, and not necessarily spiritual prodigies.

47. *Shaarey Emuna*, Shar Shelishei (Jerusalem: Raicman, 1994), chapter 5, p. 167. See Rabbi Ahron Roth (1894–1956), *Shomer Emunim* (Jerusalem: 1998), book 1, pp. 141–162, where the author records many incidents throughout history in which this idea has been demonstrated.

8
Kabbalah and Philosophy: Parallels and Distinctions

The concept of reincarnation was a widespread belief in practically every culture for thousands of years. Today it is still a native belief to many religions and philosophies. So much of the popular perception of reincarnation has been affected by these various perspectives that much confusion has resulted in regard to the Torah's view on this ancient, yet relevant, belief. In the following chapter I will juxtapose the views of the Eastern/Western-Secular with the Torah perspective, drawing parallels and distinctions. Henceforth, I will refer to all views other than those of the Torah as "philisophical" whereas the Torah's view is "kabbalistic." The distinction is that "philisophical" is a creation of intelligence, a rational, logical conclusion drawn by the human mind, and "kabbalistic," is a "received" revelation from the Divine.

THE PHILISOPHICAL PERSPECTIVE

There are those who maintain that reincarnations can only occur within one's immediate family or amongst relatives. When a soul returns again to this world to inhabit another human form, it will return as the soul of one of its relations from its previous lifetime.[1]

THE KABBALISTIC PERSPECTIVE

According to the Kabbalah,[2] *gilgul kaful*—double reincarnation (whence two souls inhabit one body), and *ibbur*—impregnation[3]—are only possible when both souls, the soul that reincarnates and the soul into which it is reincarnated, stem from the same source in the body of Adam. For example, they both have their source in the "hand of Adam."

Everything in the physical realm is a direct manifestation of its spiritual dimension. The way that something exists in the spiritual worlds above is the manner in which it will reveal itself in this physical world below. Thus, souls that are spiritual kin will also be related on this physical earth. *Gilgul kaful* and *ibbur* do indeed occur only in relatives. However, this is not necessarily the rule for reincarnation in general.

The Kabbalah speaks of a "common" reincarnation that occurs between physical relatives, and regards the mitzvah of *Yibum*. The Torah says[4] a man whose brother had died and

---

1. Ian Stevenson, *Twenty Cases of Suggestive Reincarnation* (New York: American Society for Psychical Research, 1966), p. 195.
2. See *Safer Shar HaGilgulim*, Hakdamah, 30.
3. See chapter 5, for a lengthy explanation of this subject.
4. *Deuteronomy*, chapter 25, verse 6.

left no offspring has a mitzvah to marry his brother's widow and have a child with her, so that the name of his brother "... shall not be erased." Literally, this means, that the child she will bear will preserve the legacy of the man's deceased brother. The Kabbalah, however, takes this to mean[5] that in such a case, the deceased brother's soul will reincarnate into this child, born to the living brother and his widow.

PHILISOPHICAL

There are theologians who say[6] that reincarnation occurs immediately following a person's death. The deceased person's soul will instantly reincarnate into a child who is being born. There are others who believe that it will reincarnate into a child who was conceived at the precise time of the person's death. Nonetheless, they agree that the process of reincarnation occurs immediately following the body's demise.

Others believe[7] that reincarnation of the soul occurs 100 years after a person's death. However, they concur, that when a person is killed, or dies at a young age, his soul will reincarnate into another human form immediately after his body's tragic death.[8]

---

5. *Safer Shar HaGilgulim*, Hakdamah 29, toward the end. Rabbi Yitzchak of Acco, *Meirat Einayim*, Parshat Bereishit 4:1, Rabbi Menasha Ben Israel, *Nishmat Chayim*, Maamor 4, chapter 7. Rabbi Nachman of Breslov (Jerusalem: Toraht HaNetzach, 1997), *Likutei Moharan*, part 1, chapter 21:6.

6. Ian Stevenson, *Twenty Cases Suggestive of Reincarnation* (New York: American Society for Psychical Research, 1966), p. 243.

7. Dr. Brian Weiss, In an interview in *Omni*, April 1994.

8. Ian Stevenson. *Twenty Cases Suggestive of Reincarnation* (New York: American Society for Psychical Research, 1966), p. 242.

KABBALISTIC

According to the Kabbalah, the distinct "personality" of each soul receives its reward or punishment immediately after the body's demise. Hence, the other parts of the soul, the unelevated compartments, descend below immediately to inhabit a new life. The personality of the soul of *Tzadikim* and wicked people[9] also descends immediately following death. As soon as a person dies, his soul reincarnates into children conceived at that moment. As explained in Kabbalah,[10] the Godly soul enters the body at the time of conception.

PHILOSOPHICAL

There are those who believe that there is physical continuance between reincarnations.[11] A person who was stabbed to death will have a scar on the body into which he reincarnates. They also maintain that, oftentimes, the actual appearance of the previous incarnation will reincarnate in conjunction with the soul, so that one would physically resemble one's earlier existence. Moreover, even the individual mannerisms and gestures of the previous incarnation will occasionally reincarnate into the next life. Thus,

---

9. *Safer Shar HaGilgulim*, Hakdamah 22. Rabbi Moshe Corodovero writes in Shiur Komah (chapter 4, p. 167) that there is no definitive time a soul must reincarnate.

10. *Shulchan Aruch HaRav* (Second edition), end of chapter 4. See Rabbi M. M. Schneerson. *Likutei Sichot* (New York: Kehot Publication Society, 1981), vol. 10, Parshat Lech Lecha, p. 45. The entrance of the Godly soul is at the time of conception, even though the internal connection is at the time of birth. See chapter 1, footnote 19.

11. Ian Stevenson. *Twenty Cases Suggestive of Reincarnation* (New York: American Society for Psychical Research, 1966), p. 167.

not only is there a spiritual and mental continuance from one incarnation to the next, sometimes there is even a physical connection.

KABBALISTIC

The Torah perspective regarding this issue of physical continuance is as follows. As mentioned in an earlier chapter, there is a type of reincarnation called a *gilgul kaful*, a double reincarnation, in which a soul descends into another living body—with a pre-existing soul. The Kabbalah states[12] that if in its previous incarnation it inhabited the body of a cripple, then this soul will also be reincarnated only into another body that is crippled. However, this only occurs with a *gilgul kaful*, which is not the common form of reincarnation. In the usual case of *gilgul*, whence the soul that reincarnates becomes the only soul of the new body, the Kabbalah does not state clearly that there is any physical continuance from one incarnation to the next.

The Kabbalah does, however, allude to this issue[13] in its mention of Rabbi Shieshet. Rabbi Shieshet was a great talmudic sage who was blind.[14] The Kabbalah states that the reason he was blind was because he was a reincarnation of another talmudic sage, Bava Ben Buta, whom, as the Talmud tells us,[15] was blinded by the cruel authorities of the land of Israel.

This seems to be a case of physical continuance from one

---

12. *Safer Shar HaGilgulim*, Hakdamah 4.
13. *Safer Shar HaGilgulim*, Hakdamah 36.
14. See Talmud. *Berachot* 58a.
15. Talmud, *Bava Batra*, 3b.

reincarnation to another. However, it is far more likely that it is not indeed so. Rather, the soul that was incarnated from Bava Ben Buta into Rabbi Shieshet was likely a soul that was fashioned in such a way that it caused blindness. The soul of a person who is physically handicapped is in no way less complete than that of a healthy individual. Rather, the energy of his soul is more concentrated in other areas, causing these energies to be more intense than in other areas of that person's anatomy.

The Chassidic Master, the Yismach Moshe (Rabbi Moses Teitelbaum), used to say[16] that the reason for the birthmarks on his body, which resembled stripes, was that in a previous existence he was incarnated into one of the sheep of our forefather Jacob, whose bodies, the Torah tells us, were striped.

Notwithstanding the above statements, these cases of returning birthmarks are not an ordinary occurrence, and, generally, birthmarks and wounds do not carry over from one reincarnation into the next. In the case of the Yismach Moshe, it was not a regular case of *gilgul*. A standard situation of *gilgul* is from one human being into another, and not from animals into humans.

In an earlier chapter we established that there is no continuance of personality or memory from one incarnation to the next. The distinct personality of the soul that reincarnates, is as if alive for the very first time. Although it inhabited a previous human form, nonetheless, since it had only existed in an unrevealed fashion, and was deep in the subconscious, in a sense it had never truly existed. This clearly

---

16. See Jiri Langer, *Nine Gates To The Chassidic Mysteries* (New York: Behrman House Inc., 1976), p. 167.

indicates that there is no continuance between incarnations, including a physical one.

PHILISOPHICAL

There are those who believe[17] that there is an intellectual perpetuation from one reincarnation to the next, namely, when people act *instinctively*, it is because of a subconscious memory from their previous existence. They are reacting to an experience from an earlier incarnation. For example, even little children will instinctively know to keep away from a burning flame. Not only do they turn away when they feel the heat of the fire, even before they are close enough to actually feel the heat, they will automatically withdraw from the fire. Those who say that there is an intellectual continuance between incarnations claim that these instincts come from subconscious memories, i.e., people naturally keep away from fire because deep in their subconscious they remember that fire is dangerous. Furthermore, they believe that there is also a continuance of emotions, to the extent that at times there is even a continuance of talent.[18]

KABBALISTIC

According the Kabbalah, these natural instincts of man can be traced back to the very essence of the soul. The soul,

---

17. See for example, Geoffrey Hodson, *Reincarnation: Fact or Fallacy* (Wheaton, Illinois: The Theosophical Publishing House, 1967), p. 43.
18. Dr. Brian Weiss, in an interview in *Omni*, April 1994, p. 26.

by its nature, has "traits and character." It is explained that the very nature of the animalistic soul is to animate and give life to the human body; therefore, innately, the soul wishes to stay with the body and, thus, naturally will recoil upon contact with a burning flame, which it knows can extinguish the body's existence.[19]

(There is a theory that speaks of a collective consciousness, which can be passed on from one generation to the next through DNA, and such, which may also explain human instincts.)

The abovementioned holds true with all the inborn talents of man. Kabbalah explains[20] that a person's mind is originally shaped and formed for its particular abilities. For example, there are those whose minds are shaped in such a way that they can paint beautifully, and others whose minds are formed for an inclination toward mathematics.

When a soul first enters the body of a man to animate it, the soul is already possessed of mental shape and form. There are those whose souls are "shaped" for abstract thinking, while others are "shaped" to think practically. There are brains that are actually shaped to think abstractly, while others are formed to think practically, as has been proven, observing the left and right hemispheres of the brain. Because body and soul are analogous to one another, a soul that is shaped to think in a certain way will inhabit a brain that is inclined accordingly.

---

19. Rabbi M. M. Schneerson, *Likutei Sichot* (New York: Kehot Publication Society, 1987), Vol. 25, Parshat VaYigash, p. 264. See also Rabbi Nisan ben Reuven, *Derashot HaRan* (Jerusalem: Mochon Sholom, 1977), Derush 10.

20. Rabbi Shalom Dovber, the fifth Chabad Rebbe. *Safer HaMaamorim 5666* (New York: Kehot Publication Society, 1973), p. 78. See also by the same author, *Samach TiSamach*. 5657.

There are those whose souls are fashioned to be more inclined toward *Chesed* (kindness) while other souls are molded for *Gevurah* (might). Some have the talent for arts while others have the talent for music. From the abovementioned, it is understood that instincts stem, not from some deep subconscious memory from another life, rather, from the very nature of one's soul.

Rabbi Hayim Vital wrote[21] of himself that in his previous incarnation he was a sharp-minded person and would learn everything with all its complexities, therefore, these forms of studies do not excite or interest him anymore. Now he studies in a more relaxed, complacent fashion.[22] Since the part of his soul that was connected with sharp-mindedness had already been elevated and transformed to holiness (through studying the Torah with sharpness); therefore, he will not contain these particular areas of his soul, rather, he will contain and exercise the compartments that were not yet elevated. He does not study with sharpness, not due to memory of his previous Torah study, rather, because he now has to elevate other divisions of his soul.[23]

---

21. *Safer Shar HaGilgulim*, Hakdamah 38.
22. Even though he writes (*Ibid.*) that his soul was a new soul, who descended for the very first time, nonetheless—as explained in Chapter 4, toward the end—together with his own unique soul, descended other souls.
23. As explained before (at the end of Chapter 5), Rabbi Hayim's soul (not the souls that descended together with his soul, but his own unique soul), was a new soul that was not at all elevated. When it entered Reb Hayim's body, it was the very first time it descended. Thus, how can we say that these compartments of the soul (sharpness of the mind) have been already elevated in a previous existence? It seems that it was not Reb Hayim's own soul that he was talking about when he said in his previous existence he studied with sharpness. It was someone else's, one of the other souls that dwelled within him.

Thus, from the Kabbalistic perspective, it seems that there is no continuance.[24] According to the Kabbalah, each reincarnated soul that descends upon this earth is as a newly born soul, alive for the very first time.[25]

PHILISOPHICAL

There are theologians who maintain that souls tend to reincarnate in groups, meaning, that a group of people in a previous lifetime who were acquainted with one another, will reincarnate together (friends are truly forever; they go from one lifetime to the next).

KABBALISTIC

In the Kabbalah, there is no definitive statement either way; however, Rabbi Hayim Vital does write[26] that his master, the AriZal, said, regarding his generation, that it is the same generation—the same group of souls—that were exiled in Egypt. From this statement, it may be possible to conclude that groups of people do tend to reincarnate together.

---

24. See, however, Rabbi Yoseph Caro, *Magid Mesharim* (Jerusalem: Orah, 1960), Parshat Lech Lecha, p. 14, where it seems to indicate otherwise.

25. Rabbi M. M. Schneerson, *Likutei Sichot* (New York: Kehot Publication Society, 1972), vol. 7, p. 123, speaks of a talmudic sage whom at the age of 13 (or according to some opinions 16 or 18) was as knowledgeable as a 70-year-old (see *Berachot*, 12b). The Rebbe explained that this sage inherited his knowledge from his ancestors (genetically, or through a good deed) by offering this as explanation, and not explaining it as *gilgul*, for example, by saying that he was a *gilgul* of a previous Talmudic sage. It would seem to imply that there is no continuation in intellect with *gilgul*.

26. *Safer HaGilgulim*, Sader HaGilgulim, chapter 12.

PHILISOPHICAL

"Hostility at first sight."[27] There are some who believe that the reason that people sometimes experience a feeling of immediate dislike upon meeting a new person, is because these people were individuals who were enemies in a previous existence and the hostility carried over from one reincarnation to the next.

The Kabbalah states,[28] when two souls stem from the exact same source in the "body of Adam," they will immediately and instinctively experience hostility toward each other when they meet on their life's journey. The reason for this is because each soul wishes to elevate more than the other; each desires to bring nearer to God the greater number of divine sparks. Although most people do not know the source of their souls, the soul itself is in touch with its source, and the hostility that the soul experiences upon seeing the other soul with the same source extends to the body. The Talmud touches upon this matter[29] in regard to a vision that was shown to a prophet. It was shown exclusively to the prophet, yet it had an effect on the people around him. The Talmud explains that, "Even though they themselves did not see the vision, their souls 'saw' it."

However physical the hatred may seem, it is indeed a spiritual hatred. However, once a person begins to hate, even for good and holy reasons, it will, more often than not, lead to *un*-Godly hatred.[30] It is a spiritual jealousy, for each soul wants to elevate more than the next. It is not unlike twin

---

27. Dr. Brian Weiss, in an interview in *Omni*, April 1994, p. 26.
28. *Safer Shar HaGilgulim*, Hakdamah 20.
29. Talmud, *Megillah* 3a.
30. See Talmud. *Pesachim* 113b. *Tosefot* Ad loc.

brothers, each attempting to gain more attention from their parents; thus each one endeavoring to behave and conduct himself better than the next. There is a talmudic saying,[31] "Jealousy of scholars increases wisdom." Each scholar attempts to outsmart his contemporary, to develop new and more innovative ideas. Their jealousy creates a positive effect. Jealousy is commonly the source of hate. As a wise man once observed, one only hates a person he cannot conquer. Being jealous of another means admitting that he is better than oneself. The jealousy stems from the fact that one realizes that he will never reach the other person's level. However, the jealousy that one Torah scholar experiences toward another will not lead to hatred, for it is a spiritual jealousy and will only result in a spiritual heightening. Therefore, although we find mentioned in the Kabbalah the notion of enmity, it is not a physical, unGodly hatred, rather, a purely spiritual animosity.

Furthermore, this hostility, of which the Kabbalah speaks, is not animosity that extends from one incarnation to the next (as others maintain), rather it is an innate hatred, stemming from the very source of their souls.

PHILISOPHICAL

According to Eastern tradition, it is possible for the soul of a male, namely, a soul "designed" and shaped to inhabit a male form, to reincarnate within the body of a female, or vice versa. The majority agree, however, that such transferences

---

31. Talmud. *Bava Batra* 21a.

are infrequent and unlikely.[32] However, there are those who disagree. They believe[33] that the transference of souls between genders is quite a common occurrence.[34] Due to these inter-transplantations, it is possible for a person of one gender to have features of the opposite one.[35]

KABBALISTIC

Within the Kabbalah, the idea of interchanging of the genders within reincarnation is not mentioned in regard to reincarnation for the sake of elevation. However, as explained previously, there are also reincarnations as forms of punishment (often, such reincarnations are from humans beings into lower creations), and regarding these types of reincarnations, the Kabbalah does mention the idea of interchanging of the genders.

The Kabbalah states[36] that a male who had sinned by acting like a female[37] (for example, by engaging in prohibited sexual relationships[38]), may be punished/refined through its reincarnation into a female body. This is a severe punishment,

---

32. Ian Stevenson. *Twenty Cases of Suggestive Reincarnation* (New York: American Society for Psychical Research, 1966), p. 130.
33. Dr. Brian Weiss, in an interview in *Omni*, April 1994, p. 26.
34. Master Masahisar-Goi. *God and Man* (Japan: Byakko Press, 1990), chapter titled "Questions and Answers," session 5.
35. Ian Stevenson. *Twenty Cases of Suggestive Reincarnation* (New York: American Society for Psychical Research, 1966), p. 179.
36. *Safer Shar HaGilgulim*, Hakdamah 9.
37. See *Leviticus*, chapter 18, verse 22. "And with mankind thou shalt not lie as with womankind; it is an abomination."
38. *Safer HaGilgulim*. Sader HaGilgulim. Ma-Asie Noraim.

for the shape of the male soul does not fit the female body. Therefore, the soul cannot fully express itself.

The Kabbalah explains[39] that these women who have souls of males cannot give birth, because, in order to give birth, one needs more than a female body, one must also possess a female soul. Being that these women do not have female souls, they cannot give birth.

There is a way, however that it is possible for a woman with a male soul to bear children and that is, through a departed female soul's impregnation into her body, thus giving her the ability to bear a child.[40] The Kabbalah maintains that when she gives birth, this child will be female, for the female soul that was impregnated into the mother and gave her the capability of childbirth, will now reincarnate into her child. This female soul will now become the soul of her little girl. Therefore, a woman with a male soul will only have one child, for after she gives birth, the soul that gave her that ability is no longer within her (it is now in her child).

Nevertheless, it is also possible for her to give birth through a miracle, or if she has tremendous merit. Then, she may bear many children through a soul of a departed female impregnating into her body after each birth and, thus, giving her the ability to bear another child.

Furthermore, the Kabbalah says[41] it is also possible, although very rare, for these women to give birth to a boy. This can only occur when the female soul that was impregnated into the mother's body ascends from her body at the time of birth, allowing the soul of a male to become the soul of this newly

---

39. *Safer Shar HaGilgulim*, Hakdamah 9. Rabbi Avraham Azulay, *Chesed LeAvraham*, part 5, chapter 20.
40. See *Ibid*.
41. See *Ibid*.

born boy. However, once again, it must be emphasized that this is not the norm and a female body possessed of a male soul will most likely not bear children and if any, it will be one female.

Until this point, we were only speaking of male souls inhabiting female bodies (for the process of punishment and not for *Tikkun*). What of female souls reincarnated into male bodies?

The Kabbalah explains,[42] that generally the souls of women do not reincarnate. As it is stated in Kohelet,[43] "A generation comes and a generation goes, while the earth stands forever." This statement according to the Kabbalah, alludes to the concept of reincarnation. "A generation comes and a generation goes," refers to the souls of males, who come and go, to and from this world in a constant succession of reincarnations. "The earth," which corresponds to female souls[44] (the feminine as the receptive[45]), "stands forever"— does not return to this lowly world. Once a female soul has lived even once upon this earth, it will not have to return again, it can rest forever in paradise, *Gan Eden*.

There are many questions that are immediately evident upon the above explanation. They are as follows: if the souls

---

42. See *Ibid.*, Hakdamah 9. See also Rabbi Avraham Azulay, *Chesed LeAvraham*, part 5, chapter 20. Rabbi Yeshayah Halevi Horowitz, Shnei Luchot Habrit. *Shallah HoKodesh*. HaGahot LeSafer Bamidbar Devarim. Ki Tetze. See, however, Rabbi Menasha Ben Israel, *Nishmat Chayim*, Maamor 4, chapter 19.

43. *Kehelet*, chapter 1, verse 4.

44. Rabbi Shneur Zalman of Liadi, *Likutei Torah* (New York: Kehot Publication Society, 1996), Parshat Bamidbar, p. 5b.

45. This universe was created with the equilibrium of male (masculine, the creative) and female (feminine, the receptive). (The Yin and Yang, as the East calls it.) See, Talmud. *Bava Batra* 74b. *Zohar*, volume 1, p. 157b. Thus the earth, which *receives* kernels and water, in order for the growth of trees and fruits, corresponds to the concept of female (receptive).

of females do not reincarnate, do we understand this to mean that all 613 compartments of the soul were elevated in one lifetime? How is this possible? Even were it possible, there are certain *mitzvot* that a woman cannot fulfill, being that they are percepts specific to a male. How, therefore, can her soul be completely elevated? How is it at all possible for a woman to elevate all 613 compartments of her soul? As illustrated above, it is near impossible for a person to elevate all 613 parts of the soul in a single lifetime.

The most obvious explanation is that women were given less commandments than men,[46] and, therefore, it is more plausible that a woman would elevate in a single lifetime, all the corresponding divisions of her soul.[47] However, being that a female soul possesses 613 comparmtments as does the male, the question remains: How do women elevate all 613 compartments of their soul?

In the grace that follows a meal, there is a blessing that reads, "And for Your covenant which You imprinted upon our bodies." This refers to circumcision. In the code of Jewish law[48] it states that women can participate in and say this blessing even though women are not circumcised because when it speaks of the creation of man, the Torah states,[49] "Male and Female he has created them," which essentially means that male

---

46. There are 248 positive *mitzvot* and 365 negative *mitzvot*. Women must heed all (except three) the negative commandments, and perform all positive commandments, that do not have the boundaries of time. Talmud. *Kedushin* 29a.

47. See Rabbi Moshe Edin, *Tifferet Moshe*, Darush, Le'Eishet Chayal, p. 45. The reason why women do not reincarnate, is because they have fewer *mitzvot*. Therefore, they probably fulfilled all *mitzvot*—with great caution, intensity, and fervor—in one lifetime.

48. See Rabbi Yoseph Caro, *Shulchan Aruch*, Orach Chayim, chapter 187:7.

49. *Genesis*, chapter 1, verse 27.

and females are really one singular creation, one being.[50] Therefore, women can also say, "and for your covenant . . . upon our bodies," for their male counterparts are like an extension of their own existence. And, therefore, as it says in Kisvei Kabbalah,[51] when a male does a mitzvah that the female is exempt from, he performs the mitzvah for his female counterpart as well, and it is as if she herself had performed this mitzvah. The Talmud states,[52] "A man's wife is like his own body." And the Zohar explains,[53] that each individual person, male or female, is considered to be half a body, with half a soul. Therefore, what the male accomplishes benefits the female, and vice versa.

This seems to resolve the issue of the 613 compartments of a woman's soul being elevated even though the female has fewer *mitzvot*. A male can accomplish these elevations for their female counterparts. When a husband does *mitzvot* that are only applicable to males, not only is he elevating his own soul, he is also elevating his wife's (or future wife's) soul as well.

However, this answer still leaves us puzzled, for how can we say that a female can elevate all 613 compartments of her soul in one single lifetime? Even if, as mentioned above, her husband performs certain *mitzvot* for her, and she does others, it is still nearly impossible for anyone to complete 613 elevations in one lifetime. As mentioned earlier, it is exceedingly rare that a person would complete all elevations of all souls in a single incarnation, and only a few select people ever

---

50. Talmud. *Eruvin* 18a. See also *Zohar*, Parshat, Bereishit, on chapter 1, verse 27.
51. See *Taamei Hmitzvot* by the Ari Zal. Parshat. Bereshit: Shar MaAmarei Rashbei. LeTikunei Zohar. Tikkun 69.
52. See Talmud. *Menachot* 93b.
53. See *Zohar*, part 3, p. 7b, 109a.

truly accomplish this. How is it possible that a female would elevate all the levels of soul with all its compartments in one single lifetime, when a man, doing the same as she, must reincarnate many times to achieve the same effect?

The Lubavitcher Rebbe, Rabbi M. M. Schneerson, once explained,[54] in regards to a woman's obligation in the performance of *mitzvot*. There is a verse in Exodus,[55] "This is what you shall say to the household of Yakov." The Midrash explains,[56] God told Moses to teach the daughters of Israel the *general principles* of the Torah prior to teaching the Torah with all its details to the men of Israel. The Rebbe elaborates: the women were first in receiving the Torah and were instructed in the general principles of the Torah without the details, for women are, in a sense, even more closely connected with the Torah than men. Women are in touch with the inner essence of the Torah, with the general idea of Torah. Men require the details so as to be connected. A man must perform the minutia of the law in order to become more Godly, while a woman can make a connection with God in a manner that goes beyond details. Men are required to don a *tallit* and tefillin to reach the inner essence of the Torah and to reveal their love and reverence for God,[57] while women can express their love and reverence without these external paraphernalia. Men require "tools" to bring forth their spiritual feelings toward God, while women are by nature more

---

54. See Rabbi M. M. Schneerson, *Likutei Sichot* (New York: Kehot Publication Society, 1992), Vol. 31, Parshat. Yitro, p. 93.

55. *Exodus*, chapter 19, verse 3.

56. See Midrash. *Mechilta on Shemot*. Exodus, Parsha 19, chapter 3.

57. Which is the essence of all *mitzvot*, as the Torah declares. See: *Deuteronomy*, Parshat Ekev, chapter 10, verse 12. See also Rambam, *The Guide to the Perplexed* (Jerusalem: Mossad Harav Kook, 1977), part 3, chapter 32.

spiritually attuned and can be aroused to spiritual feelings toward God, without any physical "tools."

The method in which women elevate all 613 compartments of their soul is through the observance of the general principles of the Torah, with tremendous caution, intensity, and fervor. And through observing these general *mitzvot*, which encompass the minutia of the *mitzvot*, one is able to elevate all 613 compartments of her soul which correspond to the 613 precepts.

These general *mitzvot* which we speak of are made up of six all inclusive *mitzvot* in of the Torah,[58] which are, to name a few, believing in God, loving and revering God, and so on. Women are naturally apt in these areas and tend to excel on these precepts.[59]

Women, generally, do not reincarate, and as such it would seem that a female soul reincaranted into a male form would be impossible. Nevertheless, legend has it[60] that the Shaloh HaKodesh, Rabbi Yeshayah Ben Avraham HaLeivi Horowitz (1570–1630) (הלוי ישעיה בך ארהם) was a reincarnation of the soul of Ruth (the great-grandmother of King David). The book of Ruth itself alludes to this fact. Every verse in the book of Ruth begins with the Hebrew letter Vov (ו) except for eight verses that begin with the Hebrew letter Yud (י), Shin (ש), Hei (ה), Bet (ב), Alef (א), Ayin (ע), Yud (י) and Lamed (ל), which spell out the name of this great man (הלוי ישעיה בן אררהם).

---

58. See the introduction to the *Chinuch*. (1) Believing in God. (2) Not believing in any other forces. (3) Believing in God's unity. (4) To love God. (5) Revere God. (6) And not follow the animalistic instincts.

59. Rabbi Menachem Mendel, the third Chabad Rebbe. *Yahel Or Tihilim* (New York: Kehot Publication Society, 1984), p. 435.

60. "Sader Hadorot" (Jerusalem: 1957), p. 252. Rabbi Chayim Yoseph Dovid Azulai: "Shem HaGedolim," Yud: 399.

It would seem from this legend that there is an interchange of genders from a female soul into a male body. However, from this story alone, we cannot bring absolute proof for such transformations. One could argue that the soul of Ruth was originally the soul of a male.

Generally there are no reincarnations of female souls, even from one woman to another. This is specifically regarding reincarnations that every male must go through; that is, reincarnation as a process of continuous elevation. However, reincarnation as a form of punishment, or refinement, whence a soul descends to a body into which it does not belong, may be experienced by women as well. A woman's soul can be trapped in a male's body for a sin committed in a previous incarnation.[61]

It is unusual, however, there are sometimes reincarnations of female souls. As mentioned previously, in the case of a woman with a male soul, a female soul can impregnate her and later become the soul of her child. There can also be *gilgul* of female souls when—and this is quite common—a wife reincarnates to be with her destined husband (as will be explained in the following paragraphs).

PHILISOPHICAL

Another belief in regard to reincarnation is[62] that people experience love at first sight because in their previous incarnations they had been lovers. Hence, they fall in love without all the difficulties commonly experienced.

---

61. See *Tikunei Zohar*, Tikun 70, 132b.
62. See Dr. Brian Weiss, in an interview in *Omni*, April 1994, p. 26. Geoffrey Hodson, *Reincarnation: Fact Or Fallacy* (Wheaton: Illinois: The Theosophical Publishing House, 1967), p. 44.

KABBALISTIC

According to the Torah, it is quite the opposite. If a person falls in love easily, "love at first sight" without any difficulties at all, it is proof that it is the very first time these two souls descended upon this earth, and both these souls are part of a single unified soul. As explained above, husband and wife are in essence one body, with one soul. True "love at first sight" is not because they were lovers in a previous lifetime, on the contrary, it is because this is the very first time these two souls are meeting in a physical form.[63]

The Talmud teaches[64] (at the time of conception), 40 days prior to the formation of a child, a heavenly voice declares who will be this person's destined soul mate. Every single individual has his or her destined one, his or her predestined match, known in Yiddish as *Bashert*.

The Talmud elaborates and says that a person can have more than one partner. There can be a first and second match ("second," meaning multiple—anything more than one). The first match is one's true soul mate, a part of one's very soul, while the second match one receives according to one's deeds. If one is a righteous human being, then he will also marry a righteous person; if one is a kind person, he will merit to marry a kind person, and so on.

The definition of "first" and "second" does not necessarily mean chronologically—that the first marriage was to one's first match and subsequent marriages are to one's second

---

63. *Safer Shar HaGilgulim*, Hakdamah 20. Rabbi Avraham Azulay, *Chesed LeAvraham*, part 5, chapter 20. Rabbi Yeshayah Halevi Horowitz, *Shallah Haodesh*. Shnei Luchot Habrit HaGahot LeSafer Bamidbar Devarim. Ki Tetze. Rabbi Yakov Emdin, *Yavetz*. On Talmud. *Sotah*, 2a.
64. Talmud. *Sotah* 2a. *Sanhedrin*. 22a. See also Talmud, *Moed Katan* 18b. *Midrash Rabbah, Genesis*, Parsha 68, chapters 3, 4.

match. Rather, first and second refer to quality and rank. It is possible for one to marry one's first match after one was already married to the second match.[65] For the definition of first and second is not in time, rather, in source, "first match" meaning the first in rank and quality, one's truly destined other half.[66] The only way for one to know for certain if one's spouse was truly their *Bashert* is in hindsight. If one's marriage was a healthy and successful one, one can then say that one's spouse was his true soul mate.[67]

PHILISOPHICAL

Many theologians also say[68] that if two people were married in a previous lifetime, then they will return again to this world together, in a place and time where they can eventually meet, and become husband and wife once again.

KABBALISTIC

According to the Kabbalah, this is usually the case though not always. Husbands and wives remarry in every reincarnation, as I will explain shortly. However, it does not always have to be this way. For example, a man who in his previous lifetime was married to his *Bashert*, and committed a terrible sin, may have to reincarnate into this lowly world, without

---

65. Furthermore (see the Kabbalah teaches see *Zohar*, Parshat, Bereishit, in the beginning, and Parshat, Tazria, in the beginning) that it is even possible for a person to go through his entire life and never find his true soul mate.

66. See *Zohar*, Parshat Mishpatim, Razin DeGalgultah.

67. Rabbi Avraham Azulay, *Chesed LeAvraham* part 2, chapter 65.

68. Geoffrey Hodson, *Reincarnation: Fact or Fallacy* (Wheaton, Illinois: The Theosophical Publishing House, 1967), p. 12.

his pre-destined wife. His punishment is that her soul does not descend together with his soul. The punishment is not the actual reincarnation, the fact that his soul must reincarnate. We are speaking of a *gilgul* for the process of *Tikkun* (elevation), which almost every male soul has to go through. The punishment is, that his wife's soul does not reincarnate with him.[69] (Although most female souls do not need to be reincarnated, nevertheless, as we will explain shortly, they usually do reincarnate.)

Furthermore, the Kabbalah states[70] that even in a case in which the male sinned and, consequently, does not deserve to be with his pre-destined soulmate in this lifetime, it is still possible for his wife's soul to reincarnate again and become his wife in order to spiritually assist and guide him.

However, in the usual situation, one does not commit a terrible sin, and deserves to be with his pre-destined wife. When the male's soul descends upon this lowly universe in order for it to reach its proper *Tikkun*, his female soul mate will reincarnate together with him and be his wife until he reaches his complete elevation.[71]

When soulmates descend for the first time, their souls recognize each other immediately and the transition from separate souls to a single unified soul is easily achieved. However, in the following reincarnations this transition will not be as smooth.[72]

---

69. See *Zohar*, part 2, p. 106. Rabbi Avraham Azulay, *Chesed LeAvraham* part 5, chapter 20.
70. *Safer Shar HaGilgulim*, Hakdamah 8.
71. *Safer Shar HaGilgulim*, Hakdamah 20.
72. See Talmud. *Shabbat* 130a. See *Safer Shar HaGilgulim*, Hakdamah 20. Rabbi Avraham Azulay, *Chesed LeAvraham*, part 5, chapter 20. Rabbi Yeshayah Halevi Horowitz, *Shallah HaKodesh*, Shnei Luchot Habrit. HaGahot LeSafer Bamidbar Devarim. Ki Tetze.

This means that until they finally decide on marriage and actually wed, they may go through many hardships—experiencing *internal* emotional struggles and *external* conflicts.

Returning to the abovementioned statement in the Kabbalah, in which the Kabbalah states that no souls of women reincarnate, we conclude, that what the Kabbalah actually means by this is that women's souls do not need to reincarnate for the process of *Tikkun* (elevation), for a woman can elevate her entire soul with all its subdivisions in the span of a single lifetime. However, most women do reincarnate, with their completely elevated souls,[73] in order to become the wives of their predestined husbands. They will reincarnate together with their life partner, until he completes his total elevation, the complete *Tikkun*.

The poets of the world speak of true love as eternal and everlasting, this is indeed also true according to the holy Torah, in which we learn that lovers will be together on this physical universe forever (until *Tikkun* is completed).

As a poet once wrote: "I think one is always in love with something or other, the error consists in seeking in a mortal image the likeness of what is perhaps eternal."[74]

The essential attraction between male and female, may seem to be a physical, external sensation, yet it is so much more. The physical magnetism occurs because both are part of a single existence, one body and soul. A person hungers and yearns to be one with his beloved, for he wants to be unified again as one whole.[75]

---

73. Therefore, women generally are more spiritually inclined than men, for most women (today) have within them contained all three levels of on elevated soul.

74. A poem by Percy Bysshe Shelley (1792–1822). *A Concise Treasury of Great Poems* (Permabook Edition, 1960), p. 249.

75. For the English reader see Dr. Brian L. Weiss, *Only Love Is Real: A Story of Soulmates Reunited* (New York: Warner Books, 1997).

There is an ancient argument between the wise men of the world regarding what it is that attracts people to each other. How does one choose a partner? Do opposites attract, is the appeal a result of their differences? Or is it when people are alike that they are attracted to one another?[76] According to Kabbalah it is a soul connection. When two people gravitate toward each other, it is a spiritual force that compels them to unite, and ignites their passion. There is a verse in Psalms,[77] "Hungry as well as thirsty, my Soul withers from within." The Baal Shem Tov says,[78] when we are hungry for physical nourishment we assume that it is because our physical body is hungry; in truth, it is really our soul from within that hungers. It is our Godly soul deep within us which craves to elevate the physical food toward Godliness. It is a spiritual urge of the soul, hungry for elevation, that manifests itself in a physical dimension. If the hunger would remain a spiritual desire, we, as physical people, would never feel the need to eat.

The same holds true with the love and attractions one experiences toward his beloved.

One may feel at times as if these attraction are only physical, or, on a slightly more refined plane, a mental attraction. However, all these attractions are merely manifestations of an inner truth, a soul connection to the one and only soul mate, the one destined from the time of one's creation, and the one who will stand by one's side for all eternity.

---

76. See Rabbi Yitzchak Aramah, *Akeidat Yitzchak*. Parshat Bereishit, Shar 8, Parek HaChibur.

77. *Psalms*, chapter 107, verse 5.

78. Rabbi Yisoel Baal Shem Tov, *Keter Shem Tov* (New York: Kehot Publication Society, 1974), p. 50.

9
Debating Reincarnation: Common Arguments Against Reincarnation and the Response

A typical contention when speaking of reincarnation deals with the issue of free choice. A person feels that if his destiny has been decided by the deeds of his previous incarnation, there is no true free choice in their life. Everything has been decided long before he was even born. This financial status, emotional well being and so on, all have been previously ordained by another body possessing his soul. Therefore, according to this argument, there is no room for true personal achievement in one's lifetime, no driving-motivating force compelling one to higher aspirations.

According to the kabbalistic interpretations of reincarnation, each person is judged solely on the merit of his own actions and deeds. The previous incarnations have no effect on the present incarnation's reward and punishment. Each individual incarnation of the soul is considered a new being, unaffected by anything his previous incarnations had done. The positive effects of previous incarnations exist in potential only, and can be harnessed through cultivation of the soul connection. Negativity, however, has no immortality and ceases to exist with the demise of the body.

For those whose sole knowledge of reincarnation stems from Eastern thought and culture, the concept of Karma, cause and effect, seems to preclude the need for a God of justice and judgement. The belief of Karma is such that every action causes a reaction, and the deeds of a person find a reaction in the next incarnation. Therefore, to these people, reincarnation seems to be an un-Jewish concept, negating the presence of God.

Cause and effect have a fundamental role in Judaism. For every positive deed there is a positive force created in this world, on an individual level and a global level, and vice versa with negativity. However, this belief in Judaism differs greatly from the belief of Karma in that the effects of a person's actions reverberate within their lifetime and only within that span of time. When the body passes on, it takes with it the effects of its actions in this world, and the new incarnation of that same soul is born as a newborn child, a fresh sheet of paper, waiting to be filled with a new life story.

There is much resistance to the concept of reincarnation from those who believe that there is much more to life than the superficial. They feel that there are no easy answers and resent those who would give simple explanations for difficult issues in life. Reincarnation seems to afford some the ability to explain away those experiences which seem to contradict our rational thinking. When tragedy occurs with the innocent, it is because "their previous incarnation was undeserving," and when the wicked succeed, "their previous incarnation was surely a great individual." These are pat answers, and distance those who feel that these issues are not so easily resolved.

However, Judaism does not offer simple solutions to these complicated and complex issues. Although there may in some instances be truth to answers which involve previous incarnations, not one of us has the spiritual capabilities of such calculation. Even the great Moses, of whom it was said, "There was not a prophet of Moses' stature before him and there never will be another," was stymied by the suffering of the innocent and the prosperity of the wicked, and questioned God regarding it.

There are many who find the idea of reincarnation uncomfortable. They feel that it challenges their individuality, placing them in a long chain of bodies connecting to one common soul, each body a mere vessel for this same "generic" soul. They feel that their personality and attributes are unique and individual and not something which is duplicated, like some carbon copy, from lifetime to lifetime.

These feelings are valid, and true. Each person is a completely unique individual, never having existed before and never to exist again. The soul which they share with so many before them is a multifaceted soul, built of layers and layers of spiritual dimensions. Each incarnation manifests a completely unique and individual aspect of this complex soul, resulting in a new and heretofore unseen personality and spirit. Therefore, each person is unmatched and uncomparable to any person that ever lived.

Then there are those who feel that the entire concept of reincarnation is actually a metaphor (a metaphor being an image suggesting something else) they would prefer to believe that existence in a previous form and in future incarnations represents dimensions of a person's present character and being which may not be included in one's concept of self. In other words, one's existence may be much deeper and more encompassing than one may imagine and perceive in day-to-day life.

The kabbalistic masters interpret reincarnation as an actual fact and simultaneously a parable. While reincarnation truly does occur when the soul passes on, there are also dimensions of one's soul which extend far beyond our perception of reality and are more complex than the imagination.

Appendix

To the reader, this book may seem to be speaking exclusively to a person of the Jewish faith. The terminology used is unique to Jewish thought and practice. For example, in reference to good deeds, the word "mitzvah" is used. When speaking of contemplation and meditation of God's existence, the word used is "Torah." More specifically, in reference to reincarnation itself, the text refers to the 613 compartments of the soul that correspond to the actual 613 *mitzvot* that seem to be exclusive to Jewish belief and thought.

Throughout kabbalistic literature, especially Kabbalah written in medieval times, Jewish terminology is used almost exclusively. The Kabbalah seems to be speaking for the Jewish person and about the Jewish person. The reason this was so is because when the masters of Kabbalah were writing, they were directing their text to an audience that consisted exclusively of Jews, for this was their area of influence. Furthermore, even if they had the ambition to spread their teachings to the "outside world," they did not have the opportunity, being that they were persecuted and forced to live in confined areas comprised of Jewish people only.

Moreover, the persecution left them with a fear of exposing themselves and letting it be known that there was something they could contribute that was not available in the "outside world." Therefore, there is very little foreign policy within the context of Jewish law (halacha) and within its spiritual counterpart, the Kabbalah.

To cite an example of how we see this in actuality, Reb Yosef Caro (1488–1575), in his magnum opus, the *Shulchan Aruch*—the code of Jewish Law—omits a basic principle of the Torah, which is the obligation for every Jew to influence the world in the teaching of the Seven Noachide Laws, which are for mankind in general.[1] On the other hand, Maimonides,

---

1. And the reason being that Caro lived in much harsher time for Jews, just to give some historical perspective.

In the year 1522, there appeared on the Jewish arena a man by the name of David Reuveni, who claimed to be a leader from the ten lost tribes of Israel. He said that if the armies of Christian Europe are willing to fight along with the ten tribes to oust the Muslim rule of Israel, they will succeed. With these ideas, he created great enthusiasm within the Jewish community. In the year 1525, he went to meet with the king of Portugal, John III. At that meeting, he met the king's scribe, Diogo Pires, a marrano Jew who was baptized. Upon meeting Reuveni, Diogo was greatly influenced. He circumcized himself and fled to Solinica, and was from then on known as Shlomo Molcho.

It was there in Turkey (Adrianople) where Caro (who fled from the Inquisition earlier) met Molcho and became good friends. Together, they would study Kabbalah. It was there where Molcho taught Caro how through meditation he could communicate with a *Maggid* (spirit).

A few years later, in 1532, Molcho sought an audience with the king of Spain, Charles V, who was not very impressed and handed him over to the Inquisition who then put him to death. It is known how deeply moved Reb Yoseph was by this heroic act that he himself wished he would receive this sort of death.

Rabbi Yoseph Caro, *Magid Mesharim* (Jerusalem: Orah, 1960), Parshat Tzav p. 87.

living in Egypt at a time of peace for the Jews (he himself was the king's physician), includes this law as a fundamental principle in his monumental work, the *Yad HaChazakah*.

Therefore, throughout the teachings of Kabbalah, we find little reference to the non-Jew. In keeping with the basic flow of the original writings of the great masters of Kabbalah, I have also directed the terminology to refer to the Jewish person.

However, every reference to the Jewish person, throughout the book, refers directly to the non-Jew as well. For example, all mankind, regardless of their faith possess a Godly soul.[2] All people have the potential to earn a place in paradise.[3] And every person can achieve true immortality through the revival of the dead.[4]

Judaism does not encourage others to convert to its faith. Jews do not proselytize. All people are respected for who they are and what they believe. The Talmud states,[5] that if a plague attacks a city of people, even one that contains no Jewish people, the Jews must fast for the sake of the people of that city. One must respect someone else's individuality.

The Talmud speaks of righteous men, *Tzadikim*, of other nations.[6] The holiest man in the Jewish faith is the *Kohen Gadol*, the high priest. And the Talmud states that not only a Jew,

---

2. See *Avot*, chapter 3, Mishnah 14.
3. Talmud, *Sanhedrin* 105a. See Rambam, *Hilchot Melachim*, chapter 8, Halacha 11. *Rambam* Hilchot Teshuvah, chapter 3, Halacha 5. Rabbi Menasha Ben Israel, *Nishmat Chayim* Maamor 2, chapter 7. Rabbi Pinchas Eliyahu Ben Meir of Vilna, *Safer Habrit* part 1, Maamor 18, chapter 1.
4. Rabbi Meir Ben Gabbai, *Avodat Hakodesh* part 2, chapter 42. Rabbi Dan Yitzchak Arbarbanel, *Maayanei Hayeshuah*, in the beginning. See also *Midrash Rabbah Genesis* Parsha 26, chapter 2.
5. Talmud. *Tanit* 21b. See *Tur Shulchan Aruch*, Orach Chayim, 576, 3.
6. Talmud. *Chulin* 92a.

but a non-Jew as well, who strives and struggles to achieve high levels can reach this spiritual level of the *Kohen Gadol*.[7]

Every person has his own unique purpose on this earth, and each one is crucial to the spiritual and physical wellness of the world. Each person must be respected for his or her individual abilities and capabilities.

There is a fascinating account written of a Roman Catholic Frenchman, Aime Palliere (1875–1949) and an Italian Rabbi, Eliyahu Benamozegh.[8] The Frenchman sought the advice of the rabbi in regard to the proper way to conduct his life. The man desired to become a convert to the Jewish faith, and the Rabbi counseled him against this and taught him how to live a Godly life in his own destiny, the one he was born and raised into.

Although this may be true that each and every person, regardless of religion, has his unique mission and purpose, the fact still remains that the soul consists of 613 compartments, and they must all be elevated for the realization of the soul's destiny. How does a person who is not born or converted to the Jewish faith elevate all these 613 compartments?[9]

---

7. See Talmud. *Baba Kama* 38a. The Midrash asserts that all men can receive divine inspiration. *Midrash, Tana Devei Eliyahu* chapter 9. See also Rabbi Chayim Vittal, *Sharei Kedusha* part 2, Shar 2, and part 3, Shar 7.

8. Aime Palliere, *The Unknown Sanctuary*, translated by Louise Waterman Wise (New York: Bloch Publishing Company, 1928). See also Rabbi Eliyahu BenAmozegh (1823–1900), *Be'Shevilei Mussar* (Israel: Mossad Harav Kook, 1966).

9. There are seven Noachide Laws that apply to all mankind. They are the prohibition of theft, homicide, illicit sexual relations, eating a limb from a living creature, idolatry, blasphemy, and the obligation to do justice.

These laws encompass many subdivisions of laws, which are actually part of the 613 *mitzvot* of the Torah. For example, justice includes the obligation of appointing judges and law enforcers in one's community, to inquire diligently into a witness' testimony, not to take bribes, etc.

And so, through the seven Noachide Laws, it is possible to elevate most of the soul's compartments.

The Torah itself contains the body and the soul, the law and the spirit of the law, the spiritual dimension of the physical action.

Some *mitzvot* are only done on a spiritual plane and need no physical action to achieve them (for example, the obligation to love God and fear Him). These *mitzvot* apply to all mankind. There are also *mitzvot* that are an actual physical deed, which it seems would not include non-Jews (for example, the mitzvah of tefillin, the obligation to bind one's hand and head in leather straps connected to the words of the *Sh'ma* written on parchment). However, there is a spiritual side to the mitzvah. What is accomplished spiritually through this action is the subjugation of one's mind and heart to God. Without this spiritual dimension, the actual physical deed of times accomplishes nothing.[10]

A non-Jew is also obligated to subjugate his heart and mind before God; however, this need not be done with the physical act of tefillin, rather on a purely spiritual plane.[11]

In conclusion, all people have the ability to elevate their soul in its entirety, through the spiritual dimensions of the *mitzvot* of the Torah, although not every person is required to physically do the deed of the mitzvah.

---

10. See the commentary by Rabbi Yoel Sirkes (1561–1604) *Beit Chadash*, on *Tur Shulchan Aruch* Orach Chayim, chapter 25.

11. The Midrash, *Tana Devei Eliyahu*, chapter 7, tells that a Jewish person is judged above by his physical actions, while a non-Jew is judged by his thoughts.

Index

Abarbanel, Dan Yitzchak, 24
Aderess, Shlomo Ben, 23
Afterlife, 63–77
  God-human relationship and, 71–72
  infinity and, 68–70
  resurrection, 68
  reward and punishment, 63–68
  truly new souls and, 73–74
  wicked souls, 75–77
Age level, Kabbalah study, 9
Akiva, 10–11, 145
Albo, Joseph, 24
Anaxagoras, 27
Animalistic soul. *See* Physical body

Animals
  reincarnation and, 22–23
  reincarnation as, reward and punishment, 89–93, 97
Anski, S., 116
Aristotle, 17, 27

Baal Shem Tov, 143, 181
Bahir, 12–13, 14–15
Bava Ben Buta, 161, 162
Benamozegh, Eliyahu, 190
Blood, soul and, 29–30

Caro, Yosef, 188
Character, soul and, 27
Chassidus. *See* Dovber, Shalom

Chayim of Brisk, 121
Child prodigies,
   reincarnation, evidence of, 153–155
Children, reincarnation, evidence of, 142–144
Choice, reincarnation and, 24
Comte, Auguste, 28
Consciousness, soul and, 30–31
Creation
   elevation and, 53
   Hei and, 5–6
   physical body and, 43–44
   reincarnation, evidence of, 151
   soul and, 36–37
   soul's descent and, 50–53
   truly new souls, 58–61

Descartes, René, 28
Divine law
   importance of, 7
   Kabbalah and, 7–8
   mitzvah and, 8–9
   spirituality and, 3–5
Dostoyevsky, Fyodor, 119, 120
Double reincarnation, described, 107–108
Dovber, Shalom, 72

Eastern philosophy. *See also* Kabbalah/philosophy compared
   Kabbalah perspective compared, 168–169

previous reincarnations
   evidence of, 139, 150
   memory of, 130–131
Einstein, Albert, 146
Elevation
   creation and, 53
   reincarnation, evidence of, 151–152
   reward and punishment, 84
   soul's descent and, 56–58, 61–62
Emdin, Yakov, 126
Emotion, soul and, 27–28, 31–32
Empirical evidence, of reincarnation, 140
Evidence, 137–155
   child prodigies, 153–155
   factual/empirical, 140
   religious/ideological, 137–140
   soul's descent, 152–153
   Torah, 140–142, 151–152
Evil, God-human relationship, reincarnation, evidence of, 144–151
Evil inclination, necessity for, 32
Evil spirits, *dybbuk*, 115–123

Factual evidence, of reincarnation, 140
Forgetfulness. *See also* Memory
   previous reincarnations, 127

reward and punishment, 83–84

Gender differences, Kabbalah/philosophy compared, 171–176
God-human relationship
  afterlife and, 71–72
  evidence of reincarnation, 137–140
  Kabbalah and, 17
  mitzvah and, 8–9
  reincarnation, evidence of, 144–151
  reward and punishment, 79–105. *See also* Reward and punishment
  soul and, 33–34, 37–38
  soul's descent and, 54–56
  spirituality and, 3–5
  Torah, 1–2, 9
Godly soul
  compartments of, 35
  descent of, 49–62
  selflessness and, 34

Hei, creation and, 5–6
Horowitz, Yeshayah Ben Avraham HaLeivi, 175
Hypnosis, memory, of previous incarnations, 128–129

Ibbur. See Impregnation concept
Ideological evidence, of reincarnation, 137–140
Illness, previous reincarnations, memory of, 134–135
Immortality, of soul, 38–47
Impregnation concept
  dybbuk, 115–123
  ibbur, 108–115
  previous reincarnations, memory of, 133–136
Infinity, afterlife and, 68–70
Innocence, reincarnation, evidence of, 142–144
Intellect
  emotion and, 28, 32
  soul and, 27, 31, 32–33

Jewish mysticism. *See* Kabbalah
Josephus, 17
Judah HaChassid, 41

Kabbalah
  age at study of, 9
  Divine law and, 7–8
  reincarnation and, viii–ix, 12–24
  resurrection and, 46
  spirituality and, 3, 11–12

INDEX

Kabbalah/philosophy
compared, 157–181
Kabbalist perspective,
158–159, 160, 161–
166, 169–176,
177–181
philosophical perspective,
158, 159, 160–161,
163, 166, 167–169,
176, 178
Karaites, 29–30
Korach, Moses and, 5–7
Kuf, Korach and, 6

Law. *See* Divine law
Life-threatening illness,
previous reincarnations,
memory of, 134–135
Love at first sight, Kabbalah/
philosophy compared,
176–181
Luria, Yitzchak, 12, 14
Luzzatto, Moshe Chaim,
144

Maggid of Miezricz, 152
Maimonides, Moses, 4, 20,
43, 45, 46, 188–189
Marriage, Kabbalah/
philosophy compared,
176–181
Meditation, previous
reincarnations, memory
of, 132–133

Memory. *See also*
Forgetfulness
of previous incarnations,
125–136
reward and punishment,
83–84
Menashe Ben Israel, 97
Mendel, Menachem, 26
Mitzvah
Divine law and, 8–9
reward and punishment,
65–67, 72
soul and, reward and
punishment, 84–87
Moses, Korach and, 5–7
Moshe de Leon, 13, 14
Mozart, W. A., 154
Mysticism. *See* Kabbalah

Objectivity, subjectivity and,
7

Palliere, Aime, 190
Pascal, Blaise, 28
Philosophy. *See* Eastern
philosophy; Kabbalah/
philosophy compared
Physical body
creation and, 43–44
resurrection and, 46
soul and, 25–27, 29, 30,
32
Pinchas of Koritz, 93
Plato, 18, 27, 46, 47

Possession, *dybbuk*, 115–123
Punishment. *See* Reward and punishment
Purification, soul's descent and, 53–54
Pythagoras, 18

Rapopurt, Solomon (Anski, S.), 116
Rashi, 41
Reincarnation
　arguments for and against, 183–186
　evidence of, 137–155
　　child prodigies, 153–155
　　factual/empirical, 140
　　God-human relationship, 144–151
　　innocence, 142–144
　　religious/ideological, 137–140
　　soul's descent, 152–153
　　Torah, 140–142, 151–152
　forms of, 107–123
　　double reincarnation, 107–108
　　dybbuk, 115–123
　　ibbur, 108–115
　immortality and, 47
　Kabbalah and, 12–24
　memory and, 125–136
　reward and punishment, 63–68, 79–105. *See also* Reward and punishment
　of souls of wicked, 75–77
Religious evidence, of reincarnation, 137–140
Resurrection
　afterlife, 68
　physical body and, 46
　reincarnation and, 23
Reward and punishment, 79–105
　afterlife, 63–68
　animal, reincarnation as, 89–93, 97
　elevation, 84
　forgetfulness, 83–84
　forms of, 79–81
　immortality and, 42
　materialism, 82
　reincarnation, 23, 101–105
　righteousness and, 88
　sin, 88–89, 101
　soul and *mitzvot*, 84–87
　stone, reincarnation as, 92, 96, 97–98
　vegetation, reincarnation as, 98–100
Righteousness, reward and punishment, 88

Saadiah Gaon, 20, 21–23, 30, 143
Schneerson, Menachem M., 142, 174

Schopenhauer, Arthur, 28
Selflessness, Godly soul and, 34
Sex differences, Kabbalah/
    philosophy compared,
    171–176
Shieshet (sage), 161, 162
Shimon Bar Yochai, 13
Sin, reward and punishment,
    88–89, 101
Soul
    afterlife of, 63–77. *See also*
        Afterlife
    blood and, 29–30
    character and, 27
    consciousness and, 30–31
    creation and, 36–37
    descent of, 49–62
    emotion and, 27–28, 31–32
    God-human relationship
        and, 33–34, 37–38
    Godly soul, 34–35
    immortality of, 38–47
    intellect and, 27, 31, 32–33
    levels of, 28–29
    physical body and, 25–27
    reward and punishment
        manifestations of, 94–96
    mitzvot and, 84–87
    reincarnation, forms of,
        101–105
    will and, 28
Soul's descent
    creation and, 50–53
    elevation and, 56–58
    God-human relationship
        and, 54–56
    purification and, 53–54
    reincarnation, evidence of,
        152–153
    Tikkun and, 61–62
    truly new souls, 58–61
Spirituality
    God-human relationship, 3–5
    Kabbalah and, 3, 11–12
Stevenson, Ian, 134
Stone, reincarnation as,
    reward and punishment,
    92, 96, 97–98
Subjectivity, objectivity and, 7
Supernatural, previous
    reincarnations, memory
    of, 131–132

Taitellboum, Moses (Yismach
    Moshe), 162
Tikkun, soul's descent and,
    61–62
Tolstoy, Lev, 119
Torah
    God-human relationship, 1–2, 9
    reincarnation evidence,
        140–142
Truly new souls
    afterlife and, 73–74
    soul's descent, 58–61

Universal soul, reward and punishment, reincarnation, forms of, 101

Vegetation, reward and punishment, reincarnation as, 98–100
Vilna Gaon, 89
Vital, Hayim, 15–16, 58, 100, 104, 107–108, 118, 130, 165, 166

Weiss, Brian, 135
Wicked, reincarnation of souls of, 75–77
Will, soul and, 28
Women, Kabbalah/philosophy compared, 171–176

Yismach Moshe (Moses Taitellboum), 162

Zalman, Schneur, 26, 109
Zohar, 13–14

About the Author

Rabbi DovBer Pinson was born and raised in Brooklyn, New York. He attended the Yeshiva Oholei Torah and went on to study in the Yeshiva Toras Emes in Jerusalem where he received his *semicha* from prominent rabbis and *poskim*. He returned to the States where he began to travel on behalf of Chabad outreach programs. He served as rabbi for the Jewish community in Kobe, Japan and still returns there to visit occasionally. Rabbi Pinson is currently studying in Kolel. He lectures and writes on Jewish mysticism, philosophy, and history. This is his first book.